INDUSTRIAL SOCIETY AND ITS MUSEUMS

1890–1990

INDUSTRIAL SOCIETY AND ITS MUSEUMS

1890–1990

Social Aspirations and Cultural Politics

Edited by B. Schroeder-Gudehus
With the collaboration of E. Bolenz and A. Rasmussen
Centre de recherche en histoire des sciences et des techniques
Cité des sciences et de l'industrie, Paris, France

 harwood academic publishers
Switzerland · Australia · Belgium · France · Germany · Great Britain
India · Japan · Malaysia · Netherlands · Russia · Singapore · USA

Harwood Academic Publishers

Private Bag 8
Camberwell, Victoria 3124
Australia

3-14-9, Okubo
Shinjuku-ku, Tokyo 169
Japan

58, rue Lhomond
75005 Paris
France

Emmaplein 5
1075 AW Amsterdam
Netherlands

Glinkastrasse 13–15
O-1086 Berlin
Germany

820 Town Center Drive
Langhorne, Pennsylvania 19047
United States of America

Post Office Box 90
Reading, Berkshire RG1 8JL
Great Britain

Originally published in French in 1992 as La Societé industrielle et ses musées 1890–1990 by Éditions des archives contemporaines, Paris
© (1992) by Éditions des archives contemporaines, Paris

Library of Congress Cataloging-in-Publication Data

La Societé industrielle et ses musées. English.
    Industrial society and its museums : 1890–1990 : social
aspirations and cultural politics / edited by B. Schroeder-Gudehus :
with the collaboration of E. Bolenz and A. Rasmussen.
        p.   cm.
    ISBN 3-7186-5301-X
    1. Industrial museums--History. 2. Technology--Social aspects-
-History. I. Schroeder-Gudehus, Brigitte. II. Bolenz, Eckhard.
III. Rasmussen, A. IV. Title.
T179.S6813   1993
607'.35--dc20   93-19217
                                                                                      CIP

Cover photograph © Pierre Carrere, courtesy of Cité des sciences et de l'industrie.

CONTENTS

PREFACE

ROGER LESGARDS

President of the Cité des sciences et de l'industrie, Paris, France

In March 1991, the *Cité des sciences et de l'industrie* celebrated its fifth birthday. Five years is not a very long time, too short, indeed, for historians to get much of a grip on — all the more so, given that the deliberately innovatory concept of the *Cité* owed little to any previous tradition, except perhaps Paris' long history of museums of science and technology. The *Cité* of La Villette is, in fact, very clearly the brainchild of a centralised political intelligence and will, conceived on high and imposed from above in the manner of Colbert, rather than coming into being in response to any demand from society at large.

Yet barely five years on, the *Cité* is enjoying undoubted and probably lasting success, to judge from its levels of attendance and use. Does this mean that there already existed a hidden potential demand for its services which had previously been unable or unwilling to make itself felt? It is likely that there was, if we take into account such facts as the number of families who come to the *Cité* today in order to better understand the age we live in; the way school parties use the city as an immense workshop for carrying out practical assignments; the association of industry with many major exhibitions; the willingness of scientists to come and demonstrate their work; the enthusiasm of the broadcast media for its exhibits and images, and finally, the number of imitators which the project has spawned both in France and elsewhere. No doubt those responsible for conceiving and implementing the original design had some inkling of this potential, though without fully appreciating its nature or extent. Had they allowed themselves to be unduly influenced by the often very negative reactions of some members of the scientific, academic, cultural, financial, industrial and political establishments to the project during the early 1980s, both in Paris and elsewhere in France, they would surely have abandoned the whole idea.

Perhaps this will be the principal lesson which, in decades to come, historians will draw from our venture — namely, that the public institutions in which science and technology display their wares are most often established in accordance with some only half-thought-out plan, tenaciously carried through by a few determined individuals. Such institutions then have two possibilities open to them:

- either they prove capable of evolving rapidly to meet the profound and lasting changes in social and cultural needs which have not hitherto been expressed, and through the facilities they offer, help to shape those needs,

- or they are found wanting in either the know-how or the ability to adapt to changing circumstances, and are condemned gradually to fall into a sad and painful decline.

ACKNOWLEDGEMENTS

This book has been published with the support of the Cité des sciences et de l'industrie and the Centre national de la recherche scientifique, Paris, France.

We would like to thank Graham Jones for translating Louis Bergeron's paper from French and David Chowcat for translating Wolfhard Weber's paper from German.

This volume represents a selection of papers from a collection originally published in French as *La Societé industrielle et ses musées 1890–1990* by Éditions des archives contemporaines. The source for this previous publication was a symposium held on the 14–15 March 1991, organised by the Centre de recherche en histoire des sciences et des techniques, for the fifth anniversary of the Cité des sciences et de l'industrie, Paris, France.

PATRONS AND PUBLICS :
MUSEUMS AS HISTORICAL ARTEFACTS

Brigitte Schroeder-Gudehus

Centre de recherche en histoire des sciences et des techniques,
Cité des Sciences et de l'Industrie, Paris, France

"To put things into perspective" — what better reason could there be for inviting some fifteen or so academics to speak to a varied but consistently well-informed audience about the history of museums of science and technology? "Museums of science and technology" is used in a broad sense here, to include not only conventional science museums, museums of science and industry and *écomusées*, but also those "exploratoria" and interactive science centres which, while refusing to be called "museums", nevertheless have much in common with older types of institutions. At least at the rhetorical level, almost all these institutions are committed to the spread of scientific knowledge, and there is widespread agreement as to their ultimate aim, which is to make scientific and technical knowledge readily available to all.

Whatever their origins, most museums have from the first been entrusted with an educational mission, and their history thus enables us to trace many lines of descent from the past to the present. However, we should not be misled into interpreting this history in the light of current practices as merely a slow and halting progress towards the concepts and techniques of presentation employed in today's museums of science and technology. Such an unhistorical view of museums overlooks the fact that every age and society creates museums in its own image and directs them in accordance with its own idea of the purposes which they serve.

A museum of science, technology and industry is itself a historical artefact, which reflects both the intellectual and material contexts in which it arose. The sound museological precept whereby an object should not be exhibited without reference to its social, economic and political contexts of production will here be applied to the museum itself. Among all the various factors affecting the creation and survival of museums, we have chosen to concentrate on politics in this volume. We have not hesitated to use the word in a sense very close to its usual meaning, to describe the relations between museums and the various authorities and patrons, whether public or private, on whom they depend. In doing so, however, we have deliberately avoided all the usual topics of museological debate which, without calling into question the origins and very existence of museums, have more to do with their "mission", with the conditions for the diffusion of scientific and technical knowledge, with the popularisation of science or with the norms, methods and evaluation of "museum science" in the strict sense of the term.

The creation, maintenance and development of museums of science and technology require considerable effort and financial resources. However, these resources must be obtained at the expense of other projects. It follows, therefore, that the appearance of museums of science and technology implies a certain definite wish on the part of central and local government, politicians and private financial backers to invest in this kind of institution, either in response to some more or less articulate demand from society at large, or for other reasons which will soon become apparent. This book attempts to address the questions which arise when a demand of this kind coincides with a political willingness to act upon it.

Firstly: why, in a given society, at a given moment, do museums of science, technology and industry come into being? What kind of people promote these institutions, and how do they attempt to justify them to a wider public? How should we interpret these justifications?

What are the primary considerations for those responsible for the creation of museums of science and technology? What cultural value and utility do they attribute to them? What other factors, not of a strictly intellectual or cultural order, affect their decisions?

Do museums of science and technology form part of any overall political strategy? Do they have to compete with other cultural, social or political projects? What are the decision-making processes involved?

Secondly: how does the social "need" or "demand" for such museums come into being and make itself felt? The notion of a social "need" or "demand" for museums of science and technology is far more complex and less clear-cut than would at first appear. Just like other political decisions, the establishment of a museum is usually the result of more or less complex negotiations between administrators, politicians, economic interest groups, professional lobbies and various sections of public opinion, all of whom expect that the new institution will serve their interests and give widespread currency to their own particular view of the relations between science, technology, industry and society.

Thirdly: what of the museums themselves? How do they cope with the inevitable constraints and sometimes contradictory expectations placed upon them? How much room for manoeuvre do their promoters have in negotiating with financial backers, and to what kind of controls are they subject? These are all legitimate questions, provided that we do not assume that the various protagonists form clear-cut, distinct groupings. The record reveals many affinities and overlaps between decision makers, public opinion and museum specialists, and the relations between them are best thought of in terms of loose-knit coalitions and policy communities which cut across institutional boundaries.

Nor is this at all surprising, given that the cultural heritage of science and technology is of interest to everyone and has long been the subject of deep-rooted convictions, often coupled with strong political passions. It has often been observed that cultural preferences are seldom debated, much less acted upon, without a certain militancy creeping in, and science and technology are no exception to this rule — quite the contrary.

The belief that science and technology form part of general culture, and should therefore be conserved and displayed in museums, is of quite recent origin, and even now it is doubtful whether it is universally accepted. Besides, the concept of "scientific culture" is still rather vague, while the term itself has become distinctly hackneyed. Moreover, it must be acknowledged that many fine examples of technical progress first found their way into museums as symbols of national pride rather than as outstanding cultural achievements in their own right.

It is precisely this gradual recognition of science and technology as integral parts of general culture, and thus as belonging in museums, and the numerous essays in persuasion and polemics which have accompanied this process, which makes the political history of museums so interesting.

Moreover, these controversies are still very much with us; museums of science and technology may have become *faits accomplis*, but they have laid themselves open to the accusation of having exalted scientific and technical progress while ignoring its social and political costs, of having sung the praise of industrial development while failing to acknowledge its more negative aspects and potential for conflict.

The symposium from which this work derives adopted a resolutely historical and cosmopolitan perspective, designed to bring out both continuities and parallels, and irreducible historical differences between countries and periods. Because we wanted to maintain a certain critical detachment from the institution of the museum, we have sought the opinions of historians rather than of museum theoreticians or professionals. We have not been in the business of constructing pseudo-histories or legitimating historical myths, in the manner of those so-called "historical perspectives" which delve back into the past merely in order to find congenial precedents or trace illustrious pedigrees. Rather, we have tried to bring out more clearly the distinctive character of both the institutions and the environments which sustained them.

The progressive internationalisation of current fashions in museum theory and practice might lead one to conclude that the contents on offer are also becoming increasingly standardised. However, this would be to underestimate the strength of cultural traditions and administrative practices, the extent to which museums form part of the social fabric and their dependence on combinations of institutional structures and political factors which are peculiar to each country.

We have here the basis for a genuine comparative study, though not one which underestimates the difficulties involved in gathering appropriate data and agreeing upon hypotheses to be tested. The studies which make up this collection offer more than just a handful of national case studies of museums of science and technology; they enable us to see the ways in which historical explanations differ from one country to another. The same issues do not arise everywhere, nor do they meet with identical responses. Everywhere, museums of science and technology have been symbols of national aspirations and ambitions, and their histories reflect each country's different experiences both of national pride and national despair.

Ignoring for a moment national peculiarities and at the risk of over-simplifying somewhat, one might venture to suggest that at the turn of the century, museums of science and technology were chiefly preoccupied with problems of defining and affirming their identity *vis-à-vis* more traditional institutions. During the 1920s and 1930s particularly, they became the setting for elaborate defences of economic and professional interests; and finally, from the end of the Second World War to the present, the conditions under which they exist and operate have undergone rapid and continuous change due mainly to three interrelated factors: the growth of more critical attitudes towards scientific and technical progress, the progressive absorption of museums into the leisure industry, and the ever-growing need to show positive financial returns.

No symposium or collection of papers can ever hope to find all the right answers, nor even to ask all the relevant questions. We trust, however, that in this case our combined efforts have succeeded in both enlarging and enriching the opportunities for reflection and debate.

If history can thus profit from the study of museums of science and technology, how can museums themselves benefit from a better understanding of history? And what do museum theorists and professionals stand to gain from entering into a dialogue with historians? The questions have been put; let us now begin the search for the answers[1].

Notes

1   The following articles present a selection of papers given et an international symposium held on the 14th-15th March 1991, organised by the Centre for Research in the History of Science and Technology for the fifth anniversary of the Cité des Sciences et de l'Industrie, Paris. The total number of papers given at this symposium have also been published in French (La société industrielle et ses musées, 1890-1990. Paris, Éditions des archives contemporaines, 1992).

SCIENCE, EDUCATION AND MUSEUMS IN BRITAIN, 1870-1914

Mari Williams

Agricultural and Food Research Council, Swindon, U.K.

The connections between science, education and museums have been apparent for over a century and a half to those engaged in these worlds. Debates on the role which museums can and should play in the provision of adequate science education for a wide audience have been argued throughout that time by museum curators, educationists, scientists and politicians, and may still be heard in Britain echoed in currently highly topical discussions of the public understanding of science. But it was during the half century or so before the First World War that many of the by now familiar arguments began. Those years saw the formulation of ideas about the need for and standard of scientific education in general,[1] and about the contributions that museums might make to that process. But at the same time concepts of the museum as a place of scientific display and as a centre of scientific research were also crystallising. There were therefore different tensions apparent in the debates about the function of museums; this paper will begin to explore how these tensions shaped attitudes to museums in Great Britain during the crucial years towards the close of the last century.

The main focus of this account will be the major national collections eventually housed in South Kensington, in terms of what was expected of and achieved by the grand schemes which that complex represented. But the arguments surrounding the great national centres were echoed on a smaller scale in debates on the proper role of the many local museums around the country. During the period in which we are interested the number of local museums, many including a large proportion of scientific and technological collections, proliferated, and several faced the common problems of identifying their main functions and audiences, and of finding and maintaining financial support.

But in the first instance let us concentrate upon South Kensington. As is well known, during the mid-nineteenth century this corner of south-west London became the home of Britain's national collections of scientific artefacts. The development of such a function for the region was closely linked with the beliefs and actions of the prince consort; but, although Prince Albert's name is inextricably associated with the movement which eventually brought South Kensington the Science Museum and the Natural History Museum, the arrival of each relied on strong lobbying by different groups of scientists, businessmen, politicians, artists and civil servants all with particular ideas about the need for centres at which science could be exhibited within an appropriate context. The leading protagonists, including Lyon Playfair, Edwin Chadwick and, especially, Henry Cole, were all members of the Society for the Encouragement of Arts, Manufacturers and Commerce during the period of the Prince's presidency.[2] It was from this group that the plans for the 1851 Great Exhibition emerged together with the associated notion of "a permanent home for institutions which would achieve (the) central aim of bringing science and art to bear on industry".[3] Here may be found one of the keys to the thinking of the so-called "Prince's team" which argued that, as a "peculiarly manufacturing nation", to Britain , "the connexion between art and manufactures is most important".[4] It was also vital to the prince and his associates that the public had access to this cultural connection; Prince Albert brought with him from Germany "a strong sense not only of the unity of culture but also of the public's right to direct contact with it".[5]

Following the Great Exhibition, therefore, part of the profit was invested in land in South Kensington, adjacent to the original site of the Crystal Palace. Also in the wake of the Exhibition, the Department of Science and Art was formed, significantly as part of the Board of Trade, and created in response to the proposal from the Commissioners of the Exhibition that the profits should be used for the establishment of an institution which should "serve to increase the means of Industrial Education and extend the influence of Science and Art upon Productive Industry".[6] Under the direction of the department the South Kensington Museum was opened in 1857, originally housing various of mainly non-scientific objects.[7]

Despite the rhetoric about the cultural unity of art and science and the need to display both within a suitably didactic environment, "science" was not particularly well represented during the early years of the South Kensington Museum. Anything not obviously artistic was simply gathered together as "non-art"; among these objects were foods, animal products, machinery models, building materials and educational apparatus, which included books, maps, diagrams and models. In addition, presented alongside (in the Patent Museum) was a collection of models of patented inventions and examples of industrial machinery. But these collections appear to have been regarded as peripheral to the main art collections and were inadequately housed and looked after.

During the mid-1860s, however, the Lords of the Committee of Council on Education began to take an interest in scientific and technical collections and their possible benefit to education. In 1864 the Royal School of Naval Architecture and Marine Engineering was opened in South Kensington by the Admiralty and, in association with the new establishment, a collection covering these subjects was inaugurated. Then three years later a collection of machinery and inventions was started specifically, "to afford in the best possible manner *information and instruction* in the immense variety of machinery in use in the manufactures of this country".[8]

The stage was set then for the Royal Commission on Scientific Instruction and the Advancement of Science, established in 1870 under the chairmanship of the Duke of Devonshire.[9] In the commission's fourth report, attention was turned to the scientific collections held at the South Kensington Museum. It was recommended that these should be kept, together with the Patent Museum collection and a new collection of physical and mechanical instruments, within a completely new establishment.[10] Although a subsequent offer by the exhibition commissioners to share the costs of building and maintaining a new science museum with central government was finally refused, the recommendations of the Devonshire Commission marked an important moment in the history of the Science Museum, for the *idea* of such a museum took root, and did so firmly in the context of scientific and technical instruction.

Moves towards the realisation of a national science museum were furthered in the mid-1870s, when the Lords of the Committee of Council on Education approved a proposal to exhibit a Special Loan Collection of Scientific Apparatus at South Kensington.[11] Membership of the advisory committee created to oversee the selection of objects to display illustrates the combination of interests brought to bear on the idea. Learned societies and professional institutions were represented; the Astronomer Royal George Airy and other eminent scientists, including Clerk Maxwell and Lord Rayleigh were involved, and industry was represented by, among others, William Siemens. Their intention was to display apparatus for teaching and investigation and, at the same time, objects with historical significance because of whom they were used by or the work for which they were employed.

The exhibition opened in existing South Kensington buildings in May 1876 and it was these objects which went on to become the core of the Science Museum collection.[12] The idea of a science museum as an entity in its own right gained ground during the 1880s and 1890s, with lobbying from the scientific community, especially during the early 1890s when an attempt was made to build a new art gallery on land scientists had earmarked both for a science museum and for the extension of the Royal College of Science. Once again, although much was said about the needs for adequate space and resources for the collection and display of scientific artefacts, at this time these parts of the collections at South Kensington seem often to have been regarded as the poor relations of the larger and more coherent artistic collections. Nevertheless, signs that the scientific arguments were beginning to be heard emerged at this point and the new Tate Gallery was built elsewhere in London.[13]

But still the British government refused to be convinced of the need to create a new building to house the scientific collections. Indeed at this point some parts of central government were beginning to show signs of dissatisfaction with the management of both the science and the art collections in South Kensington. Questions about the administration of the collections were asked in the House of Commons and in 1897 a select committee was established to look into administration in South Kensington and in a number of other museums under the control of the Science and Art Department.[14] Again, in considering the department's museums as a whole the science collections (now referred to as the Science Museum, although still housed in the same unsatisfactory conditions) were marginalised, illustrating either that it was felt that this part of the department's duties were being adequately performed, or, more probably, that science and scientists still had work to do to convince central government that they mattered. Whichever the reason, one of the most significant outcomes of the commission's two reports was the decision to build new housing for the art collection in the newly created Victoria and Albert Museum, and to leave the fate of the Science Museum until after this was completed.

The turn of the century witnessed the disappearance of the Science and Art Department, with its activities being taken over by the new Board of Education,[15] re-emphasising the links between museums and education. Indeed while arguments persisted over the housing of the science collections in general the development of the specifically educational functions of the science museum had been helped by the steady development of the Science Library.[16] Formally created in 1883, the new library was based upon earlier collections associated with the original education collection from the 1850s, supplemented in 1876 by the library of the Inspectors of the Committee of Council on Education and in 1883 by books from the library of the Museum of Practical Geology in Jermyn Street in central London. The links with education and scientific research were obvious: for years the library functioned as a principal resource for the Royal College of Science, continuing to do so throughout the rather fraught years (for other collections) of the late nineteenth and early twentieth centuries.

Debate on the different potential functions for the Science Museum re-emerged before the First World War, when the Bell Committee reported on the Science Museum and the Geological Museum.[17] The section of the report devoted to the "purposes the Science Museum should serve," made the following points: "the collections in the Science Museum ought to afford illustrations and exposition of the various branches of Science within its field and of their applications in the Arts and Industries. [It] ought also to be a worthy and suitable house for the preservation of appliances which hold honoured place in the progress of Science or in the history of invention... So too the Museum should serve [those] who on particular occasions wish to obtain from the Collections information regarding recent advances in Science or in Industries... Again the objects exhibited or otherwise preserved in the Museum should be accessible for close inspection by accredited visitors who are engaged upon investigations related to Science or invention."

Notably, the report went on to say, "A large proportion of those who visit a Museum have, however, no such definite enquiries in view, and it is of much importance that objects should be so selected and exhibited as to arouse the interest of these visitors, and to afford them in as simple and *attractive* a form as possible an opportunity of obtaining at least general ideas on the subjects which the Collections illustrate."[18]

The competing or complementary requirements of education, research and entertainment thus clearly mattered still in 1911, as they had for much of the history of science museums.

The question of whether and why these functions were each fulfilled maybe illuminated by considering the second major national science collection housed in South Kensington — the Natural History Museum — then, as now, part of the British Museum. As described by Nicolaas Rupke the transferral of this collection from the principal British Museum site to a new purpose-built home followed a series of intricate and sometimes heated debates in Parliament.[19] Arguments revolved around whether facilities in Bloomsbury (where the collections had been badly housed) should be extended or whether a completely new building dedicated to these particular scientific objects should be erected. Among the arguments voiced were some familiar ones. It was said, for instance, that the collections should stay in Bloomsbury to keep them "accessible to the mass of London's population"; they "presented great attractions to the working classes; and, being there those classes were gratified by the sight of other objects, by which their tastes were expanded and elevated".[20] So access to a wide public in the interests of education and of the "promotion of science and art" was important. But in addition there were economic arguments. Members of Parliament found themselves facing the question of the cost of housing the growing natural history collections, and of whether it would be more economical to transfer them wholesale to a new cheaper location in the suburbs (as South Kensington then was), rather than pay for an expensive extension in the heart of the capital. Early in the debate (that is, in the early 1860s) both Prime Minister Palmerston and Home Secretary Cornewall Lewis favoured transfer to South Kensington on grounds of long-term cost. But their measures were defeated also on grounds of cost (this time in the short term), because the creation envisaged by Richard Owen, then responsible within the British Museum for the natural history collections, was attacked as "crazy, rash and extravagant".[21]

While financial arguments dominated the debate during the 1860s, once Disraeli ousted Palmerston as prime minister, events took an unexpected turn. As Rupke points out, while possibly unhappy about the cost to the public purse of a new Natural History Museum, Owen's vision for the centre was one with which the imperialist Disraeli could identify, and his erstwhile opposition to the plan was modified. Then on Gladstone's return to power he, a long-standing supporter of Owen and his plans, ensured that the new museum was realised, opening its doors in 1881.[22]

In this episode of the museum's prehistory we can see that the economic dimension was used skilfully by both proponents and opponents of the scheme. The financial arguments might not in themselves have been decisive — but the extended argument of what was *worth* government financial investment was. It was necessary to secure the political will to put government funding at the disposal of science (in the national interest). Thus, as Rupke shows, Owen's early contact with Gladstone was crucial to the success of the Natural History Museum. Similarly, the roles of the prince consort and politicians and civil servants associated with him were vital to the South Kensington Museum. However, in the latter it was the wide cultural rather than specific scientific arguments which dominated, leaving the Science Museum less comfortably placed than either of its grand neighbours on the eve of the First World War. While the Natural History Museum was a place of education, entertainment and research by then, the Science Museum still had to win further political arguments before that could happen. The science collections in South Kensington did not have a champion comparable with Richard

Owen; nor— despite advertising British industrial achievement —did they have the imperialist appeal of the collections associated with Bloomsbury. They thus failed to attract significant political attention or related government financial investment to enable the Science Museum to develop as a source either of entertainment or of education.

This combination of economic and political problems was also faced, albeit on a smaller scale, by museums outside London, and in the provincial context once more arguments over the competing roles for a museum are encountered. In the 1870s provincial museums in particular were under attack from scientists and from within the museum fraternity itself. For example, in 1876 Boyd Dawkins, curator of the Manchester museum at Owen's College, attacked museums in Britain for being "sort of advertising bazaar(s) or... receptacle(s) for miscellaneous curiosities unfitted for a private house".[23] At this time the majority of museums were private collections in the keeping of individuals or learned societies, which were, according to Geoffrey Lewes, historian of the Museums Association, "often... of... little educational value".[24]

During the late 1870s the need for general museums reform was debated in the pages of *Nature*. F.W. Rudler, then a lecturer at the University of Wales at Aberystwyth wrote that museums should be "educational engines"; at the same time James Paton, curator of the Kelvingrove Museum in Glasgow, urged curators to be like "a newspaper editor, a man of general knowledge and culture".[25] Paton also argued for formal training for curators, and for proper financing of provincial museums: the issue of funding was particularly sensitive as the Royal Commission for the 1851 exhibition had failed to allocate any resources at all outside London. Then in 1880 A.C.G. Gunther addressed the meeting of the British Association for the Advancement of Science (B.A.A.S.) on the theme of "Museums, their use and improvement", in which he claimed that "the principal aim of a provincial museum ought... to be popular instruction." Subsequently, the B.A.A.S. formed a committee on provincial museums which, in 1887, emphasised the need to have *scientific* curators, and to change from providing "toys and hobbies" to "an adequate system of education".[26]

In the wake of the 1887 B.A.A.S. report interest among curators in a Museums Association grew and by the end of the 1880s an inaugural meeting had taken place. Among the common interests of the group were: plans for arranging natural history collections, promotion of museum lectures to working men and preparation of small educational loan collections for circulation among schools.[27] During its early years the Museums Association dealt with many issues having a bearing on the proper functions of local museums, and the debates in which they were engaged reflected those occurring at the same time in the national arena. In particular the question of resources mattered. During the closing decades of the century the number of municipal museums grew noticeably; these were dependent upon local government finances, but resources were not generous and curators found themselves having to choose between competing functions. Schemes for raising funds or other resources were high on the agenda around the turn of the century, while the Museums Association was in discussion with the Department of Science and Art over museums' grant-in-aid. Ideas included the establishment of a group of peripatetic museum specialists to supply provincial museums with expertise they might otherwise not afford; the creation of a trust to which individuals could leave their collections; and a national store of objects to be made available only to museums not housing the national collections. But at the heart of the matter was the familiar problem of investment — or subsidy — by government. During the decade before the First World War the Museums Association pressed for review of the grant-in-aid system in favour of provincial museums, and also entered into negotiations over the level of local rates museums were required to pay. The latter varied from museum to museum and was seemingly at the discretion of local government, adding to the financial burdens of those which were unable to obtain an exemption. In this and other respects then museums were at the mercy of their local authorities. The provision of buildings or space to house collections might have been undertaken by the authority, but museums had to rely on private patronage for special plans, as in the case of the extension of the Dorset County Council in Dorchester in south-west England, which became possible in 1903 only following the benefaction of local dignatory Charles Hansford.[28]

The resource concerns of local museums therefore reflected those of their national counterparts in a similar way to that in which the debates over the principal functions of museums were echoed. Moreover in both local and national contexts the closing years of the nineteenth century and the opening years of the twentieth witnessed the beginning of lobbying on a large scale in support of museum causes. The pages of national and local newspapers and journals were used to air views and call for government commitment to museums.[29] This trend may be seen as an adjunct to the contemporary attempts by particular scientists to place scientific research — as well as scientific and technical education — on the national agenda;[30] and in both campaigns the arguments have continued to the present day. Museums (especially the natural science collections) are still identified as centres where science should be explained to a wide audience, as well as places of entertainment, and the tensions which such double expectations generate preoccupy those engaged in running the institutions.[31] And, over and above the debates over primary function, the questions of funding and of the extent to which government investment is necessary remain as unresolved now as they were a hundred years ago.

Notes

1   For the most recent account of standards in scientific and technical education in England in this period see Robert Fox and Anna Guagnini (eds.), *Education and Industry in Europe, 1850-1940.* Cambridge-New York, Cambridge University Press, forthcoming. Introduction and chapter by Anna Guagnini.

2   See D.S.L. Cardwell, *The Organisation of Science in England.* Revised edition, London, Heineman, 1972, pp. 75-76.

3   F.H.W. Shepherd (ed.), *Survey of London.* Volume xxxviii. *The Museums of South Kensington and Westminster.* Athlone Press, London, 1975, p. 74.

4   *Ibid.*

5   *Ibid.*, p. 75.

6   *Second Report of the Commission for the 1851 Exhibition.* London, 1852, p.11.

7   See David Follett, *The Rise of the Science Museum under Henry Lyons.* Science Museum, London, 1978, ch. 1.

8   Quoted in *ibid.*, p. 2.

9   The minutes of the meetings between the Devonshire Commission and witnesses were published with the eight reports of the commission between 1873 and 1875.

10 *Fourth Report of the Royal Commission on Scientific Instruction and the Advancement of Science.* London, 1874, p. 23; see also Follett, *op.cit.*, 1978, pp. 2-3.

11 *Ibid.*

12 See Science and Art Department of the Committee of Council on Education, *Catalogue of the Special Loan Collection of Scientific Apparatus at the South Kensington Museum.* London, 1877.

13 Follett, *op.cit.*, 1978, pp. 6-7.

14 The Select Committee on Museums of the Science and Art Department published reports in 1897 and 1898.

15 The Board of Education was created in 1902 and, as pointed out by Peter Alter, had from its beginning, the major governmental responsibility for science education; see P. Alter, *The Reluctant Patron: Science and the State in Britain, 1850-1920.* Translated by A. Davies, Oxford, Berg, 1987, p. 6 and *passim.*

16 Follett, *op.cit.*, 1978, p. 7; see also L.R. Day, "Resources for history of science in the Science Museum Library", *British Journal for the History of Science*, 18 (1985), pp. 71-76.

17 The Bell Committee — the Departmental Committee on the Science Museum and the Geological Museum — was appointed in March 1910, with the principal aim of examining the educational and other purposes of the national collections at the two museums; see Follett, *op.cit.*, 1978, ch. 3.

18 *Report of the Departmental Committee on the Science Museum and the Geological Museum, Part 1,* 1911; Follett, *op.cit.*, 1978, p. 21.

19   Nicolaas A. Rupke, "The road to Albertopolis: Richard Owen (1804-42) and the founding of the British Museum of Natural History", in *Science, Politics and the Public Good*. Basingstoke, Macmillan, 1988, pp. 63-89.

20   See *Hansard*, CVLIII (24 April 1860) col 48; quoted in Rupke, *op.cit.*, 1988, p. 67.

21   *Ibid.*

22   *Ibid.*, pp. 71-74.

23   See Geoffrey Lewis, *For Instruction and Recreation: A Centenary History of the Museums Association*. London, Quiller Press, 1989, p.1.

24   *Ibid.*

25   Quoted in *ibid.*, pp. 3-4.

26   *Ibid.*, pp. 4-6.

27   The remainder of this section is based on *ibid.*, ch. 3.

28   See J. Gunning, "How is the design of a provincial museum influenced by contemporary opinion and specific local needs and how have these influences changed with time? Case study: Dorset County Museum", paper provided by the author.

29   In particular the pages of *Nature* were used throughout this period for arguments about the role of both national and local collections, and the level of government funding necessary for them; but the *Times* also carried accounts of the debates, as did local newspapers throughout the country.

30   On the rise of the science lobby see P. Alter, *op.cit.*, 1987, pp. 76-98.

31   Witness the recent cuts made in the research staff at the Natural History Museum and the coverage given in the national and international press; on the choices currently facing science museums see Robert Fox, "Research and curatorship in the national science museums: a reflexion on threats and opportunities", *Impact of Science on Society*, 159 (1991), pp. 263-271.

THE POLITICAL HISTORY OF MUSEUMS OF TECHNOLOGY IN GERMANY SINCE THE NINETEENTH CENTURY

Wolfhard Weber

Ruhr Universität Bochum, Germany

The foundation of every museum always has a double function:
• On the one hand, it is a political decision which expresses the cultural needs of citizens, members of Parliament or ministerial officials. It is therefore very dependent on the surrounding atmosphere, the prevailing opinions and conceptions as to the usefulness and purpose of museums or exhibitions. The decision to establish such a cultural institution not only ties up considerable funds, but also presupposes as a rule the affirmative effect of the exhibits, the much-cited normative power of the factual.
• On the other hand, such a museum, once it exerts an active influence on public opinion, acts as a landmark attracting or facilitating a new perspective. The decision-makers usually proceed on the assumption that they have set up a sign of endorsement for themselves, their retention of power and their self-image, as well as for their constituents. This fact very often provides the key to understanding the actual process of foundation.

Let us consider from this aspect the foundation of large public museums of technology devoted to the conservation and presentation of historical technology. Technology is used here in a broad sense, that is, to include the dominant scientific, cultural, social and economic interests.[1] Indeed, the historian will first call to mind the art chambers of the Renaissance and then the machines of the Baroque princes.[2] These were later supplemented by the collections of the academies and learned societies.[3] However, after the separation of the fine arts and the practical arts in the middle of the eighteenth century and the incorporation of the practical arts into the spheres of activity conceded to the business community, there was no longer any reason for the princes to collect or exhibit these "bourgeois" objects as well. Indeed, Napoleon I recognised early on that here lay a source of support for the idea of national greatness, and he arranged for commercial products to be displayed in the Conservatoire des arts et métiers from 1799 onward. The polytechnics regarded themselves from the beginning as the core of a (bourgeois) national education,[4] rather than as part of a worldwide scientific community. For these reasons, in order to promote bourgeois trade and industry, many German princes and industrial associations mounted such trade exhibitions in the first half of the nineteenth century. With the decline in wealth of the old estates, which could no longer exert such a disproportionate influence on the market, there was a concomitant decline in standards of craftsmanship where these were no longer in demand, leading to attempts at preservation in Nuremberg (Germanisches Nationalmuseum 1853),[5] as well as in Stuttgart (Landesgewerbemuseum 1852) and in Berlin (Kunstgewerbemuseum 1852). The universality of approach and the general optimistic and pacific tone are striking, until the moment when the nationalistic educational approach of the polytechnics "caught up with" the industrial museums, as Gottfried Semper pointed out at the time.[6]

13

Unlike the Paris Conservatory, which could draw on the enthusiasm for the Republic and the funds of the academy, Londoners concentrated their activities on the remains of their Great Exhibition of 1851, which were exhibited in the South Kensington Museum from 1852 onward. It must be borne in mind that there had already been considerable controversy in London in connection with the exhibition over the extent to which the claim of industry to be guarantor of the peace both internally and externally was to be represented. Faith in external peace was already shattered as a result of the Crimean War, but domestic peace in respect of the improvement of the welfare of the lower classes was, as the indefatigable Thomas Twining[7] (1806-1895) repeatedly emphasised, likewise to be allotted a special section in the exhibitions. Indeed, at least since the Universal Exhibition of 1867, Napoleon III had competed with his English rivals to devote the necessary attention to this area as well, extolled in Germany as the "opening up of the moral sphere of activity" (Reuleaux).[8]

The foundation of the German Reich in 1871 led to rapid recognition by museums of the part played by technology in this unification process. This applied initially to the inevitable weaponry (1880 in the Berlin Arsenal), which was also exalted in Bavaria and Saxony, etc. More noteworthy, however, is the Imperial Postal Museum of 1872. Recollection of the old privilege of Thurn and Taxis, which was abolished in 1867 at the time of the North German Confederation, and the putting on display of a modern, state-run postal system, which used the railways for transportation and also operated a telegraph system, was also a matter of general approval for a federal empire in the new imperial capital.[9]

At the end of the nineteenth century, the German Reich began to rely consciously on the modernity of its industry. Museum visitors were made aware of this orientation in two ways. On the one hand, there was recourse to the older generation of technical equipment. However, pioneering contributions from Germany had been few and far between. Mechanics and steam-engine technology were regarded as "English". Museum presentation therefore emphasised the railway museum, the vehicle which brought industrial technology to Germany. The nationalisation of the railways, the unusually high and important revenue for the Prussian national budget, together with the high social prestige of this technology, justified the establishment in 1905 of a Design and Transport Museum in the *Hamburger Bahnhof* in Berlin, a railway station which had been closed down in 1878.[10]

The new technologies based on the natural sciences, electrical engineering, chemistry, Zeppelins and large passenger ships could, however, be directly related to independent German achievements. An effective role could be found for all of them in museums. Three "technical" museums were therefore founded in Germany at the beginning of the twentieth century, which will now be examined in detail:

(a) in 1899, the Industrial Safety Exhibition in Berlin, later (1927) called the Arbeitsschutzmuseum;

(b) in 1903, the Deutsches Museum in Munich;

(c) in 1905, the Museum für Meereskunde (Oceanography Museum) in Berlin.

These "museums" were characterised by a mixture (typical of exhibitions) of instruction and reflection which benefits museums, but which all too often remains restricted to art museums. The mixture of instruction and reflection on display can, however, be interpreted as an expression of three politico-cultural movements:

In the case of (a) the national government and circles close to power had tried since the beginning of the universal exhibitions to emphasise the utility of industrial technology for the solution of the social question, for the provision of health and hygiene facilities. Their own exhibitions too, such as the General German Exhibition for Hygiene and Life-Saving Equipment in Berlin in 1883-1884 (reflecting the mood accompanying Bismarck's welfare legislation), which was opened to the general public in 1886 as a museum of hygiene, emphasised the problem-solving character of modern technology. A large "German General Exhibition for Accident Prevention" held in 1889 clearly and deliberately set different standards to those set by the French Republic, in 1878 in particular. In the growing struggle to sway public opinion, the German Reich wanted to make its mark in the field of welfare institutions, hygiene facilities and in all technical aspects of health, and to associate itself with the blessings of "state socialism", as Bismarck called it. This lasted until 1899, when the employees and associates of the state insurance authorities had established their right to representation against the opposition of the curators. Four years later, in 1903, the "Permanent Exhibition for Industrial Welfare" opened its doors.[11]

The ambivalence with which the engineered character of the technical environment, experienced later by contemporaries as civilisation, could be viewed and the consequences which could arise from this, can be demonstrated by the initiatives in Munich: social policy-makers and engineers from Munich (and Saxony or Baden) put forward policies propagating technically engineered health and, in 1911 in Munich, opened the Bavarian Workers' Museum, founded at the instigation of the Polytechnical Association. They thus became part of the bourgeois reform movement.[12] However, this museum, initially greeted with great goodwill, later fell out of favour with the general public as the Polytechnical Association was now giving preference to "scientific education".

In the case of (b) in 1903 (the year the industrial safety museums opened in Berlin and Munich!) Oskar von Miller, a leading electrical engineer for the long-distance transmission of electricity, instigated the foundation of a technical museum which was to be devoted not to the various branches of industrial technology, let alone their repercussions, but solely to the genesis of "masterpieces", the outstanding achievements of the technical sciences and the admiration of these. To this end, the public had to be instructed in the natural-scientific foundations of the "new" technology, an idea which Miller brought with him from Berlin, where the private society "Urania" had been successfully carrying out such a programme of public education since 1888 and where at the same time the Imperial Postal Ministry had been similarly engaged in providing information on the fundamental principles of the new technologies. Here was to be found a clear expression of the "new" technologies, which promised every individual tangible advantages from new technical products, together with the traditional claim of engineers for membership of the educated classes (recognition of the title Dr. Ing. in 1899). While the railway and naval museums were created in Berlin, in Munich Miller had won over with his concept both the Association of German Engineers and the influential Central Association of German Industrialists, both of which wished to prevent engineers "drifting away" into professional bodies close to the unions, and to whom Miller conceded a large say in the planning of the museum. After the fundamentally positive response from imperial circles, he was granted an extensive board of trustees which included the Reich's leading representatives in the new natural and technical sciences, thus minimising any potential friction. Apart from the Imperial Exchequer, these were the Imperial Physico-Technical Institute, the Patent Office, the Public Health Office, the Standard Calibration Commission, as well as the Academies of Berlin, Dresden, Munich and Göttingen. Lacking were social reformers or figures associated with the social museums who could have contributed something regarding the effects of industrial technology. So right from the beginning, the assessment of the results of scientific and technical change was placed in the hands of the instigators, whose chief demand of the younger generation was "respect" for the achievements of the older generation.

The national pantheon and hero cult inhibited for a long time any discussion as to the advances made by the innovations which had been introduced or the question of the social bases and consequences of technical activity, to the great annoyance of Emil Riedler, a professor of mechanical engineering influential in court circles, who in 1904 had demanded just such a grouping together of technical with economic and social aspects to give a cultural-historical perspective. Riedler repeated his criticism frequently and always coated in praise, as can be seen, for example, in his report on the board meeting of the Deutsches Museum of October 1905 addressed to the Prussian Minister of Education, Studt, on 9 November, 1905. His praise was directed at the pedagogic function of the museum — as opposed to Paris and London — and its qualities as a central museum. "Particularly noteworthy pieces" should therefore also be transferred from the Prussian State Collections (in Berlin) to the Munich Museum, as in the shipbuilding or transport museums in Berlin these "would never meet with such great success as they would in a uniformly designed, appropriately organised central museum". Riedler concluded: "Against the planned detailed organisation, I would raise objections to the Board in the essential respect that the economic consequences should be clearly emphasised rather than taking the scientific and historical aspects as the sole basis. I shall forward a copy of my proposals to Your Excellency in due course." If Riedler had at least some small success with his objections, there was only a negative response to the conservative fundamental critique of Oswald Spengler in his 1930 lecture "Kultur und Technik" which drew attention to the aggressive potential of the technical activities of "Man".[13] The Deutsches Museum and the Association of German Engineers were also in future quick to take up together newly emerging fields of technical identification and acceptance of historical dimensions.[14] When in the twenties the electric motor rapidly achieved acceptance in the countryside as well, the obsolete water-wheels soon became cultural monuments. In a reaction against the prevailing rationalisation, a large public discovered the cultural charms of outmoded power drives and production equipment in the Erzgebirge, the Bergisches Land, the Sauerland, etc.[15] The Association of German Engineers and the Deutsches Museum were supported in their endeavours by the *Deutscher Bund Heimatschutz* which, like the conservationists in the U.S.A., endeavoured to preserve the countryside and the small-scale rural industrial structures.[16]

In the case of (c) as the German Reich adapted to the new quality of scientifically based technology in the first decade of the twentieth century (through the founding of the Kaiser Wilhelm Society, for instance) a number of decisions had to be made regarding new museums. The Reich considered its own immediate future to lie on the sea; the Oceanography Museum was made available to the Navy for the display of imperial visions.[17]

No funds were made available during the Weimar Republic for founding new cultural institutions. Berlin, however, as a central railway junction, had been given its own museum in 1905 (just a few years after the opening of the Transport Museum in Bavarian Nuremberg in 1901). As a generation later the future of Germany appeared to lie rather in the motorisation of land and air transport, in 1936 the Aeronautical Museum in Berlin (already established during the Weimar years and aimed against the Allied prohibition on flying) was accorded a new, prominent position, and in 1937 the Deutsches Museum in Munich opened a new motor-vehicle hall.

There was one exception to the general reticence: the officials of the Mining Association in Essen. Shortly after 1918, an attempt had already begun to counteract the image of the union-loving miner and the idea of a nationalised mining industry by means of a technical folklore museum. They built on local initiatives, laid claim to the tradition of the Museum for Mining and Metallurgy, closed in 1917, for their initiative, exhibited the private teaching aid collection of the Westphalian Mining Association Treasury and, following the foundation of the Mining Museum in Bochum in 1930, placed great emphasis on the folkloric interpretation of the social processes in the mining industry. The contemporary rationalisation may also have contributed to this retrospection.[18] One may well regard it as a kind of reaction against the upgrading of the so-called "Industrial Safety Museum" in Berlin in 1927 (by a Social-Democratic Minister of

Labour), but it was also a regional decision, for in 1927 the Ruhr mining industry had equipped the German Industrial Safety Museum in Berlin with a mine for teaching purposes, and in 1928 they provided the Deutsches Museum in Munich with a mining department.

In 1945, after a total and technical war, technical culture had a difficult job to be recognised as being of value. In occupied Germany, no presentable exhibits could be obtained of the "masterpieces of natural science and technology" which had rendered such good service to the German Fascist military, or at least had been intended to do so, while many of these experts had either been forced to leave the country (for the United States or the Soviet Union) or had lost their public reputation in war crimes trials and were therefore hardly suitable as lobbyists for the provision of exhibits to museums.[19]

Thus after 1945 technical museums were initially unable to obtain culturally positive positions and consequently there was practically no funding for foundation and development. From 1955 onward, the federal government had its hands full with the nuclear programme, while the governments of the Länder were more preoccupied with the costs and provisions of the constitution, which assigned (school!) education to them and the promotion of the sciences to the federal government.[20]

Three museums were founded in West Germany in the 1960's which still bore the traces of the period before the two world wars:[21]

1. After the reconstruction years, Wilhelm Claas resumed his endeavours of the 1930's for a museum for technical cultural monuments. Looking to foreign models, the structural change in the West German Länder led to the construction of other than purely rural museums. The Westphalia-Lippe Regional Authority, responsible for museums in eastern North Rhine Westphalia, opened its Museum for Technical Cultural Monuments in 1967, although this certainly could not have been realised so quickly without the dedicated assistance of the Federal Association of German Industry and its long-standing president, Fritz Berg from Hagen. Let it be mentioned merely in passing that this idyllic museum was created in the 1960's, a time of great physical and psychological stress for the working population; to explain it as a compensation attempt as Hermann Lübbe does cannot be dismissed out of hand if one takes into consideration the working conditions of the late thirties and the early sixties and looks closely at the non-governmental initiators.[22]

2. Two further technical museums were created in the sixties or found an influential lobby; the German Shipping Museum Foundation in 1971 in Bremerhaven and the Museum of Transport and Technology in Berlin, whose actual foundation did not, however, take place until 1980.

The city of Bremerhaven, a region in a state of economic crisis (decline in transatlantic passenger shipping 1955-1960), decided to set up the Shipping Museum following a series of initiatives: a "Heimat" museum completed in 1961, the discovery of an old Hanseatic sailing ship in the Bremen city harbour, the rebuilding of the city centre by filling in the New Harbour planned as of 1962, the purchase and exhibition of the sailing ship Seute Deern in the Old Harbour in 1966, the incessant urging of the director of the local Chamber of Commerce (member of the Shipping Museum Board of Trustees 1967) and finally the repeated attempts of the maritime and art collector Dr. Hans-Willy Maria Bernartz of Cologne, who wished to leave his collection to a museum. The bad conscience of the citizens of Bremen, who now finally wanted to do a good cultural deed for their Bremerhaven appendage, was relieved when Bernartz in particular pointed to the tradition of the Berlin Oceanographic Museum and pressured the federal government into providing 50% of the finances of what was now to be the German Shipping Museum.[23]

I do not intend at this point to consider in any detail the successful private or semi-public museums which have been displaying exhibits from the transportation and communication sector (cars, aeroplanes, railways) since the middle of the seventies, and which in some cases enjoy massive attendance figures. It was they who often paved the way for the creation of public museums for technical exhibits. However, the interest of the visitors, and especially that of the children, is usually concentrated not on the social conditions of development and application, but on figures and design, on horse power, in short, on consumer dreams and wishes.[24]

3. In 1960 the Berliners were already recalling their former central transport function. It was during this year that lovers of historical transportation technology attempted to have the Design and Transport Museum in the *Hamburger Bahnhof* reopened to the public.[25] But it was not until the cultural reorientation in the seventies that the Berlin Senate recognised the role of such a museum as a cultural focus, as an educational institution and as a place of enlightenment which provided an alternative environment to the real contemporary world.[26]

A fourth "museum" with prewar traditions should also be mentioned. This is the Industrial Safety Museum, destroyed in 1944 and initially deliberately not rebuilt, only to be rebuilt after all in 1980 in Dortmund (under the Christian Democratic Welfare Minister Blum and in his Dortmund constituency) as the German Industrial Safety Exhibition (D.A.S.A.).[27] What general reasons can be given for the industrial museum boom in West Germany in the 1970's ?[28]

In their reorientation after 1945-1955 historians had been able to refer back to American, French and also German initiatives of the twenties and thirties. The widening of scientific perspectives by raising questions of social and economic history led beyond a narrow reliance on political aspects of constitutional history and gave rise to an adequate range of answers which could then be applied in the 1960's to regional or local issues. As the nationalistic perspective was also a thing of the past, after 1955 a generation grew up without heroes, and historians and politicians alike devoted themselves increasingly to questions of structure and system, but not of meaning.

The overcoming of the nationalistic perspective began only very late, at the end of the fifties. Tolerance towards regional cultures, of which there was a tradition in Germany, was now accompanied by a degree of sociocultural tolerance, which was certainly encouraged by an unprecedented increase in the number of Germans travelling abroad. From about 1960 onward a younger generation gained influence in politics and society, but they still acted too cautiously and were themselves overtaken by an even younger generation of students and journalists who gained a large degree of public approval, leading to a change of power in Bonn. This laid the ground for an opening up of the political sphere so that the social demands of workers and other underprivileged groups could now be argued out in public. Thus in the late 1960's, and especially after the student uprising of 1968, an extensive process of cultural rethinking began which at the same time was to provide a basis for an entire generation of new museums.

An important precondition for this was the recognition, however cautious, of socio-political demands which had been made since the 1950's, such as those for unions, for rights of co-determination or for graduated pensions. In this way, a basis was established for a new socio-political climate in the sixties.

The variety of lifestyles was discovered and explored with the intention that such investigation and portrayal should lead to greater tolerance. Included in this were the "charms" of the factory; everyday life; childhood; women; ecology; all those spheres which had been inadequately represented in the depictions of high culture up to that time. One notable exception was historical research into old age and death, if one disregards medical engineering. A perspective from the everyday, using methods of oral enquiry, was to open up new fields along the lines of the *"Annales"* school.

As the social-liberal coalition changed its policies towards the social situation of the workers (e.g., the action programme "Humanisation of Working Life") and supported its constituents with a series of measures, the cultural shift was also clear; the question of the cultural, and subsequently, the emotional costs of the furious reconstruction and of industrialisation as a whole was raised with ever greater emphasis. The European Year of Monument Protection fitted in with this general mood and led to redoubled enquiry into the increasing level of destruction.[29]

The second half of the seventies was occupied with the attempt to develop a new, broader cultural understanding which included the traditions of commercially employed people, and two characteristic poles emerged: industrial culture, favoured by architects and economic historians and understood largely as an extension of previous bourgeois cultural understanding, and working-class culture, whose proponents propagated a quite independent understanding which was not exactly bourgeois, but multicultural.[30]

But this alone does not explain the great success of the industrial and labour museums which constitutes part of the overall success story of museums. One factor was certainly the self-confidence of the new generation and the change in industrial structure. The post-1945 reconstruction generation, which was just stepping down, wanted recognition for their economic and social success. In the absence of a nationalistic perspective and a portrayal of the fine arts which was barely comprehensible to the greater masses, the field lay wide open for regional history and history of the *"Heimat"* — but no one wanted to venture in at first! From the standpoint of the educational initiatives of the late sixties, historians were needed in the schools and in the universities, or else believed that there was scope here for social transformation; museums were (still) considered too antiquated for such activities.

An abrupt and profound change overcame the cultural life of Germany in the middle of the seventies. Initial reactions came from the state bureaucracy, to be followed, after a change of government, by the trade associations. The oil crisis, budgetary deficits and the falling birth-rate led in Germany to rigorous cut-backs in the number of teachers, scientists and educationalists, and students were directed toward the so-called "free" market. In the search for openings, they then began to develop the above-mentioned themes and made up many cultural deficits at the local level through the expansion of museums. The rising generation grasped the opportunity for regional cultural development and took their will for social-pedagogic endeavours with them into the museums.[31] This was also backed up by the attempt to satisfy cultural demands through a greater degree of commercialisation, to which tax legislation also contributed.

All-out rivalry in matters historical now set in amongst the *Länder* and municipalities as they competed for their public image, and tourism also made its mark. Baden-Württemberg led off with a Stauffer exhibition in 1977, followed by Bavaria in 1980 with the Wittelsbach dynasty and Berlin in 1981 with the Hohenzollern one. They all documented the rekindling of public interest in individual and collective biography, approaches which had still been taboo in the sixties.[32] At the same time, however, these exhibitions also provided employment for a large number of young historians who had not yet found permanent posts.

Of all these reform efforts, life and work in industrial conditions proved of particular interest, not least because the dominance of large-scale industrial production was losing its appeal. The sole exception were the old favourites, cars and aircraft, but even these factories were carrying out fundamental reorganisations of their production. The inflexible utilisation of tools and machinery became obsolete as a result of recent advances in rationalisation using electronically controlled machine tools. Such administrative optimisation entailed a certain ambivalence (and continues to do so): on the one hand, there are those social groups who adapt rapidly and successfully to the new technologies, as they stand to gain from such unprecedented advances in production, while on the other hand there is a very diffuse group among the affluent who do not wish to see the drudgery of previous working practices given up so easily, while they too would like to show evidence of their dedication to progress and development.

While in 1966 in West Germany there was a total of 673 museums with 12.7 million visitors, the number in 1988 had rocketed to 2400 with over 60 million visitors. Technical museums are responsible for a major share of these massive attendance figures. Concrete initiatives for a wide range of museum foundations came from various directions:

(a) Many bleak, "planned-to-order" large-scale housing estates with unsociable towerblocks combined with multi-lane roadway developments, had devastated towns and cities and led to a deterioration in the quality of urban life and a lack of opportunity for people to meet. Historically interested architects and curators of monuments now strove to conserve outstanding technical buildings in order to use them as museums or otherwise give them new functions. This was an international movement (cf. the International Committee for the Conservation of Industrial Heritage); it already found expression in the policy of North Rhine Westphalia in 1970 in a governmental programme, as well as in the foundation of two large regional industrial museums in the Ruhr area (Dortmund and Oberhausen) with the specific aim of providing arenas for an expanded concept of culture.[33] Following up this initiative, architects and town planners have meanwhile devoted themselves to this region at the International Architectural Exhibition at Emscher Park and are planning a large-scale government-sponsored structural change which will preserve the industrial heritage.

(b) The parliaments of the German *Länder* and municipalities began in the mid-seventies to establish unique identities for their *Land* or region and drew on the expanded concept of culture for this purpose. Thus public platforms were created which, by setting forth "progressive" lines of development, presented an optimistic and self-assured picture of regional structural change while not forgetting Germany's international connections. In this way, the *Länder* were able to hold discussions as competent federal partners within the framework of European unification. As a consequence, questions concerning the national unification of Germany receded into the background or else were totally ignored.[34]

In September 1990 (following the announcement by Prime Minister Späth in 1978, which was prompted in turn by the proposals made by Werner Conzse's pupil, Hans Jürgen Weineck, since 1965), the *Land* of Baden-Württemberg opened a showpiece museum, the "*Land* Museum for Technology and Labour", a very costly glass construction whose very conceptual premises were determined by the State Parliament. Its contents included remnants of the Stuttgart National Trade Fair of 1896, thus providing historical continuity across the old territorial borders of Württemberg and Baden. The attractive mixture of original major pieces and aesthetically pleasing "showcases" certainly meets the requirements of the majority of visitors.[35]

In 1980, the *Land* of Hamburg commenced work on a "Museum of Labour"[36] housed in historical buildings as in the case of North Rhine Westphalia and intended as a counterpart to the Mannheim museum since it concentrates on "wage labour" and thus intends to work together with unions rather than with industrial associations. It is, moreover, not intended as a permanent exhibition, but will offer interested groups an opportunity to exhibit. Only in this way, it seems, was it possible to overcome the unyielding opposition between the political parties, as well as that within the ruling party (the S.P.D.) and the unions. We shall have to wait and see how long the supply of spontaneous groups keeps up and proves capable of resisting the professional interest of the exhibition organisers. Local efforts from the sphere of workers' culture have had a great influence on the new ways of presenting technology. Judicious and competent cultural spokesmen have produced great achievements; however, Hessen has had a hard time with an industrial museum up to now.[37] Solely the municipality of Rüsselsheim with its museum designed by Peter Schirmbeck has already taken account in exemplary fashion of the traditional social and the more recent ecological challenge of industrialisation, whereby it profited from the Frankfur museum experiments.[38]

Pioneer work at the local level and in scientific preparation was carried out notably by the city of Nuremberg, in this case with the sponsorship of *Kulturdezernent* Hermann Glaser. The Centre for Industrial Culture was established very early on (under the directorship of Wolfgang Ruppert and then Hans Jürgen Sembach) and set new precedents in the presentation of issues linked to industrial and workers' culture, repeatedly attracting public interest with new and worthwhile exhibitions.[39]

At the beginning of the eighties, the German public was shaken out of this retrospective, popularising sensibility, which testified to a renunciation of great national goals and which was displayed by a multitude of smaller groups as well as by the "alternative" movement, and which reflected a pronounced impulse of West German social criticism, finding expression in the "retreat" into local history and in history workshops. Young people abandoned the traditional parties, their elders had become more conservative, and the economy, after a decade of profitable foreign investment, now sought to invest once again in Germany, which also meant following the example set by both West and East and investing in armaments. Wealth and pomp were socially acceptable once more. In the ensuing reorganisation, considerable sums were placed at the disposal of large theatres and museums. The return of a national perspective with the incorporation of the German question into that of Europe also made itself felt during the centenary celebrations of social insurance legislation, in which the German welfare state was looming large in the new museums.[40] Public educational institutions as part of the foundations of cultural activity now fell out of favour, to be replaced by tax-deductible financing through trusts and labour contracts. One of the main aims of this industrially oriented policy was to combat an alleged antagonism to technology.[41]

The result was not only two different concepts of culture existing side by side, but also two different types of museum. In cases where a Conservative state government decided on a technical museum, an architectural showpiece or a space travel department (as in Munich) demonstrated a positive presentation of industrial technology; in *Länder* ruled by Labour parties, former factories served as crystallisation points for the presentation of our industrial-cultural heritage, in which the democratic demand for citizens' participation was also to have its place. A large exhibition (in North Rhine Westphalia) on industrialisation planned in conjunction with the dynasty exhibitions fell victim in the 1983-1984 recession to the cuts imposed by the S.P.D. The same fate was met by an exhibition which was to feature Düsseldorf as the metropolis of shipping on the Rhine.[42] Precisely in the case of these two exhibitions, it might well have been more important for the municipalities to have prevented large sums being drained off by such showpieces from their own budgets. The nationalistic turn[43] of the Bonn government gave rise in the early 1980's to two major historical museums in Germany which were intended to present a meaningful image of Germany after fifty years of the Federal Republic: one in Bonn for the early years of the new Republic, and one in Berlin for the overall assessment of Germany in Europe, the antithesis of the East Berlin Museum for German History, as it were. Both integrated the social, economic and technical aspects in a political context, albeit in the form of set pieces and political affirmation rather than with regard to the ecological questioning of the meaningfulness of our excessive use of technology and striving for growth or the social consequences of our wealth in the form of migrations of other nationalities or minorities due to poverty. National politics have once again overtaken technology.

At the present time it is totally unclear whether the collapse of the G.D.R.[44] will lead to the conservation of the many technical museums or technical monuments maintained until now by industrial *"Kombinate"*.[45] As things stand, the self-confidence of the new *Länder* ought not to remain inhibited for long. Above all, the great potential for unrest of the many dismissed intellectuals must be diverted toward a new and satisfying task. But it remains to be seen whether this cultural unrest will lead to new industrial and labour museums, which cannot be presented as evidence of a successful economic or technical policy, but would rather have to make do with the attributes of a collapsed socialist economy, bearing the stigma of the creators of the present misery. It is indeed questionable whether the new citizens will be able to come to terms with their former Stalinist power structure via an analysis of a past era of industrial technology. Even if the (West German) social consensus of 1949, which deferred demands for reform in favour of the benefits of economic growth, were to be repeated in the ex-G.D.R., it cannot be guaranteed that the change in perspective on cultural policy which took place here in 1968 will also come about there.[46]At the present time, a harking back to the "pre-Republic" era is observed in the Eastern*Länder*.[47]

Notes

1   Günter Ropohl, *Eine Systemtheorie der Technik*. Berlin,1982.
2   Detailed work has already been done on the art chambers in Kassel, Dresden, Berlin, Braunschweig-Wolfenbüttel and Stockholm. For an overall view: Bruce T. Moran, *Patronage and Institutions. Science, Technology and Medicine at the European Court 1500-1750*. Woodbridge, 1991.
3   Friedrich Klemm, *Geschichte der naturwissenschaftlichen und technischen Museen*. Munich, 1973.
4   W.L. Volz, "Über höhere Polytechnik", *Polytechnische Mitteilungen 1* (1844), pp. 1-6.
5   Veneration of the Middle Ages and the mediaeval Empire and regret at the loss of many mediaeval art treasures following the Major Resolution of the Imperial Deputation of 1804 formed the cultural-political background to the foundation.
6   Utz Haltern, *Die Londoner Weltausstellung von 1851*. Münster, 1972, p. 328.
7   Wolfhard Weber, *Technik und Sicherheit in der deutschen Industriegesellschaft 1850-1930*. Wuppertal, 1986, p. 25 sq.
8   See Weber, *op.cit.*, 1986, p. 27 : In Mülhausen/E. a tradition of welfare institutions (Industrielle Gesellschaft) had already been in existence since 1826; frequently cited, it came, however, to an end in 1895 for political reasons.
9   Bavaria, with its own postal service, set up its Postal and Transportation Museum in 1901 in Nuremberg. Discussion regarding the inclusion of technology in museums thus goes back considerably further than the date of the founding of the Deutsches Museum in Munich would indicate. The Prussian and German capital, Berlin, did not, however, opt for a central museum, but favoured individual museums for different sectors, branches of industry, etc.
10   Alfred Gottwaldt and Holger Steinle, *Verkehrs- und Baumuseum Berlin. Der "Hamburger Bahnhof"* Berlin, 1984.
11   See Weber, 1986. It is striking that the *Reichstag* (or more specifically in this case, the objections of the Conservative party) did not allow the Ministers of the Interior, Berlepsch and Bötticher, who were suspected of being supporters of reform, to set up such a museum.
12   Already in 1882, in parallel with the Berlin initiatives, the Polytechnical Association wished to set up a welfare exhibition devoted to industrial safety and hygiene. See *1815-1915. Hundert Jahre technische Erfindungen und Schöpfungen in Bayern*. Jahrhundertschrift des Polytechnischen Vereins in Bayern. Munich, 1922.
13   See Oswald Spengler, *Der Mensch und die Technik*. Munich, 1931. Citation from Federal Archive Merseburg Rep. 76 V G 1 X 6, Vol. 1, pp. 158-160, and Rep. 120 E VI 16, pp. 230-231. In the field of historiography, Friedrich Klemm, librarian at the Deutsches Museum since 1932, has provided a framework for the consideration of such views with his cultural-historical interpretations of technology. On the foundation of the Deutsches Museum, see Maria Osietzki, "Die Gründung des Deutschen Museums. Motive und Kontroversen", *Kultur und Technik* 8 (1984), p. 6; and *eadem*, "Zur Gründungsgeschichte des Deutschen Museums von Meisterwerken der Naturwissenschaften und Technik in München 1903-1906", *Technikgeschichte* 52 (1985), pp. 49-55, esp. p. 62. The National Socialists were later to be critical of the technicistic viewpoint, as they wished to see stronger emphasis placed on nationalist and racist aspects. But even then, they were not unhappy with the concept of a (supposedly) value-free representation of technology committed to the community. See Zdenka Hlava, "1925-1945. Kleine Zeitgeschichte gesehen von der Museumsinsel in der Isar", *Kultur und Technik* 8 (1984), pp. 9-97. It should be pointed out that almost all the museums for the history of the natural sciences only deal with the era of industrial production from the aspect of technical development, and thus are fundamentally only somewhat extended museums of technical history.

This situation will have to change.

14   Conrad Matschoss, the Director of the Association of German Engineers (V.D.I.), evidently won through here against Oskar von Miller. See Wolfhard Weber, "Von der Industriearchäologie über das 'Industrielle Erbe' zur 'Industriekultur'. Überlegungen zum Thema einer handlungsorientierten Technikhistorie", in: *Technik-Geschichte*. (eds. U. Troitzsch and G. Wohlauf). Frankfurt/M., 1980, pp. 420-447; Wolfgang König, "Zur Geschichte der Erhaltung technischer Kulturdenkmäler in Deutschland" (pp. XXIII-XXVIII), and Rainer Slotta, "Zur Situation der Pflege technischer Denkmäler und der Industriearchäologie in der Bundesrepublik Deutschland. Versuch einer Bestandsaufnahme" (pp. V-XXII), both in : C. Matschoss and W. Lindner (eds.), *Technische Kulturdenkmale*. Berlin, 1932. Reprint Düsseldorf, 1984.

15   In mills, of all places, whose employees were formerly often ostracised: Werner Danckert, *Unehrliche Leute. Die verfemten Berufe*. Munich, 1963, p. 125 sq. It is remarkable what a change in perspective there has been from the image of the miller as an outlaw, living outside of the community, to that of the power station engineer as hero engaged with modern technology. Carl Schiffner, *Alte Hütten und Hämmer in Sachsen*. Berlin (Ost), 1959, and Wilhelm Claas, "Die Planung eines Freilichtmuseums technischer Kulturdenkmale in Hagen i.W.", *Technikgeschichte* 26 (1937), pp. 148-152. For a general summary Conrad Matschoss and Werner Lindner (eds.), *Technische Kulturdenkmale, op.cit.*, 1932.

16   The cooperation guidelines can be found in *Beiträge zur Geschichte der Technik und Industrie* 18 (1928), p. 145; Ulrich Linse, "Die Entdeckung technischer Denkmale. Über die Anfänge der Industriearchäologie in Deutschland", *Technikgeschichte* 53 (1986), pp. 307-320.

17   For an overall survey of the problems involved see Wolfhard Weber, "Verkürzung von Zeit und Raum. Techniken ohne Balance zwischen 1840 und 1880" (pp. 11-261) and Wolfgang König, "Massenproduktion und Technikkonsum. Entwicklungslinien und Triebkräfte der Technik zwischen 1880 und 1914" (pp. 265-552), *Propyläen Technikgeschichte*, Vol. 4. Berlin, 1990.

18   Evelyn Kroker (ed.), *50 Jahre Deutsches Bergbaumuseum*. Bochum, 1981; on the mining customs union, see Heinz Reif and Michael Winter, *Essener Zechen. Zeugnisse der Bergbaugeschichte*. Essen, 1986; Wilhelm Busch, F. Schupp and M. Kremer, *Bergbauarchitektur*. Cologne, 1981.

19   The philosopher Friedrich Dessauer did gain public attention with his idealistic theory of technology, which could provide some basis for a museum of "masterpieces".

20   For the history of education and science after 1955, see: Maria Osietzki, "Modernisierung oder Reform? Das Erbe der Wissenschafts- und Bildungspolitik der 50er Jahre", in: *Universität und Politik*. Bochum, 1991, pp. 11-54. This federal divergence is evidently responsible for the fact that there is to this day not a single science centre in Germany.

21   It is surprising that there is still no energy museum. In view of the state's close involvement with this sector, this would have seemed a matter of course. Initiatives to this end in the seventies arising from the nuclear power debate repeatedly failed, apparently because the financially strong electric supply companies approached for contributions wanted greater control over the museum's policy. They preferred exhibitions giving a positive image of nuclear power and held either in or near nuclear power plants. This public policy was also followed by the armaments business and extended to severe censure of all statements critical of nuclear power, and spread to technical museums as well wherever it was possible to exert influence there. Of late, the attitude toward cultural objectives has begun to change once more. The renegotiation of many (municipal) contracts is imminent and must be prepared for; numerous publications on the history of the power industry have appeared recently which have been financed or sponsored by the electricity companies.

22   See F.H. Sonnenschein and Chr. Kleinert, *1000 Jahre Technik- und Handwerksgeschichte*. Hagen, 1984; Hermann Lübbe, "Der Fortschritt und das Museum", in: *idem, Die Aufdringlichkeit der Geschichte*. Graz, 1989, pp. 13-29, see especially p. 29; *idem*, "Technischer Wandel und individuelle Lebenskultur", in : *idem, Fortschritt der Technik - gesellschaftliche und ökonomische Auswirkungen*. Heidelberg, 1987, pp. 49-64. This latter draws connections between the inclination to cling on to the familiar and the huge environmental changes of the last fifty years. However, this phenomenon might well be observed in the 1860's, the 1900's, and in the 1930's as well.

23   See *Das Werden des Deutschen Schiffahrtsmuseums*. Second edition. Bremerhaven, 1971.

24   Forerunners were the museums of car firms such as Daimler-Benz or Volkswagen, and later also the Bayerische Motorenwerke, who thoroughly "overhauled" all of these "show cases" in the 1980's in order to use them for sales promotion. The disproportion between these investments and those made in the company archives is (was) therefore usually extreme.

25   See Gottwald Steinle, *op.cit.*, 1984. The museum was closed and, although situated in the West, was under the supervision of the G.D.R. Reichsbahn. Financial necessity led the G.D.R. to sell the West Berlin S-Bahn and the museum to the West in 1985.

26   The Berlin Senate allocated the *Anhalter Bahnhof* area for this purpose, a site which, being so

central, would hardly have been made available after the reunification of 1990.

27 See Bundesanstalt für Arbeitsschutz, *Deutsche Arbeitsschutzausstellung*. Gesamtkonzeption March 1990.

28 The attempts made in the G.D.R. to set up technical museums focusing on cultural history and the history of productive forces have not yet been fully documented: neither have the attempts made since 1981 to establish a large "national" (decentralised) museum of technology.

29 This question was soon extended to the environment as well: Rolf Peter Sieferle (ed.), *Fortschritte der Naturzerstörung*. Frankfurt/M., 1988.

30 Hermann Glaser (ed.), *Industriekultur in Nürnberg. Eine deutsche Stadt im Maschinenzeitalter.* Munich, 1980; Gerhard A. Ritter (ed.), *Arbeiterkultur.* Königstein, 1979; research project by Werner Conze *et al.* on the social history of the labour force. This tradition was superseded by research into the middle classes, appropriate to the change in the national political climate

31 Typical book titles include: E. Spickernagel and W. Walbe (eds.), *Das Museum, Lernort contra Musentempel.* Giessen, 1976; and Andreas Kuntz, *Das Museum als Volksbildungsstätte. Museumskonzeptionen in der Volksbildungsbewegung in Deutschland zwischen 1871 und 1918.* Phil. diss. Marburg, 1976.

32 Signs of change were indicated in 1973 with Joachim C. Fest's biography of Hitler.

33 Influential in initiating this political change was the Düsseldorf M.P. Karl Heinz Bargmann, who died prematurely in a motoring accident. The machine shop at Zollern 2.4, which now forms the nucleus of the Dortmund Industrial Museum, was preserved from demolition in the nick of time by the well-established and vigilant German Mining Museum in Bochum; see *Ein Westfälisches Industriemuseum.* Münster, 1979; *Das Westfälische Industriemuseum.* Münster, 1985; *re* the Oberhausen Industrial Museum, see *Rheinisches Industriemuseum.* Cologne, 1984; *Tatort Fabrik — Das Rheinische Industriemuseum im Aufbau.* Cologne, 1989. For cultural activities in old factory buildings, see Richard Grübling *et al.* (eds.), *Kultur aktiv in alten Gebäuden.* Berlin, 1979. For a resumé of industrial-cultural activities, see the journal *Tendenzen* No. 159 (July 1987).

34 Its continuing relevance following the collapse of the Stalinist power structure in Eastern Europe is evident. The great majority of commentators in the culture industry were taken totally by surprise by the collapse of government and society in the G.D.R., a fact certainly attributable to the continued existence of two cultures and the lack of perspicacity of many public spokesmen in matters of technical and social processes or the basis of the social consensus which underlies highly differentiated industrial societies.

35 *Stationen des Industriezeitalters im deutschen Südwesten. Ein Museumsrundgang.* Stuttgart, 1990. The public observed the development of the museum's conception: see Werner Raith, "Kritische Fragen sind nicht erwünscht", *Basler Zeitung* of 30.6.1984.

36 Gutachten Museum der Arbeit. Hamburg, 1986.

37 After the critical response to the didactic museum of the 1960's, Frankfurt now hopes to gain a reputation as a city of culture with a whole series of prominent museums. Evidently, the chemical industry was considered unsuitable for increasing environmental consciousness and for a spectacular major museum, as was the nuclear power industry, which now receives intensive support in Hessen, that one-time paragon. The metropolis Frankfurt has now been equipped by a C.D.U. municipal government with all the blessings of a culture intent on aestheticisation and the display of wealth. In view of the recent constitutional amendment officially establishing Frankfurt as the German federal banking centre, it will be very interesting to see how the industrial past will be presented. Meanwhile, a private association is attempting to set up an industrial museum there; the same applies for Hanover.

38 Peter Schirmbeck, *Industrialisierung.* Rüsselsheim, 1975; *Idem, Orbis Pictus Naturae. Eine Bilderfibel zu Mensch und Natur.* Bonn, 1990.

39 See H. Glaser *et al.* (eds.), *Museum und demokratische Gesellschaft.* Nuremberg, 1979. Sembach had already stimulated wide public interest with two large exhibitions: the exhibition on the occasion of the 125th anniversary of the foundation of the Association of German Engineers, held in Berlin in 1981 (Tilmann Buddensieg *et al., Die Nützlichen Künste.* Düsseldorf, 1981), and the exhibition celebrating the 150th anniversary of the introduction of the railway to Germany, held in Nuremberg in 1985 (*Zug der Zeit - Zeit der Züge. 1835-1985. Eisenbahnen in Deutschland.* 2 vol. Berlin, 1985). The Berlin exhibition in particular paid great attention to the *mise en scène*. Nuremberg also distinguished itself with a comprehensive exhibition on the Industrial Age (the only one of national significance on this subject so far): Gerhard Bott (ed.), *Leben und Arbeiten im Industriezeitalter.* Stuttgart, 1985.

40 E.g. Wolfgang Mommsen (ed.), *Die Entstehung des Wohlfahrtsstaates in Grossbritannien und Deutschland 1850-1950.* Stuttgart, 1982.

41 The Georg Agricola Association for the Promotion of the History of the Natural Sciences and Technology — the Society for the Promotion of the Deutsches Museum, established 1928 — thus

developed plans in 1981 for a multi-volume *Cultural Encyclopaedia of Technology*, which has since started to appear. There are no plans for a volume on antagonism to technology. Whether the initial intention is successfully realised can only be assessed following publication of the concluding volumes (Economy, Society and Technology).

42 See the contributions in *Neues Bergisches Jahrbuch*, Vol.3 (1990), edited by B. Dietz.

43 For a protest against the nationalistic turn from the pen of a defender of the social museums and workers' culture: Wolfgang Ruppert, "Zwei neue Museen für Deutsche Geschichte? Vorschläge zu ihrer demokratischen Öffnung", *Geschichte und Gesellschaft* 12 (1986), pp. 81-92.

44 The East Berlin Museum for German History was an initial victim of this collapse.

45 The German Museum Federation drafted an appeal for the preservation of at least the most important industrial monuments in Winter 1990-1991.

46 See Lutz Niethammer (ed.), *Bürgerliche Gesellschaft in Deutschland*. Frankfurt/M., 1990, p. 515 sq. However, as regards museums, I envisage initially a common trend in both parts of Germany away from the objects of everyday life and toward a higher evaluation of aesthetically pleasing exhibits. This may also be reflected in the foundation of science centres in which classes in physics and chemistry can be held, as state schools in both East and West are increasingly unable to provide adequate laboratory facilities and the demand for basic education in the natural sciences is extremely great. The Berlin Museum for Transportation and Technology is already going in this direction.

47 I should like to thank Evelyn and Werner Kroker of Bochum for their assistance and suggestions.

THE CITY AS A MUSEUM OF TECHNOLOGY

Miriam R. Levin

Case Western Reserve University, Cleveland, Ohio, U.S.A.

Histories of technology museums in France usually begin with the founding of the Conservatoire national des arts et métiers in 1794 during the most radical phase of the Revolution. Housed in a converted monastery, this institution had its roots in Enlightenment ideals regarding the educational value of technology collections. It was established by decree of the Convention to encourage French artisans and craftsmen to study the latest machinery in order to improve French manufacturing. The founders' goals were political and economic. Practical education at public expense offered skilled workers an opportunity to contribute to their own and the new Republic's welfare by making French products competitive with those of its rivals.[1]

Quietly, and not unintentionally, there appeared another museum of technology in France during the Revolutionary period: a living museum, with constantly changing exhibitions, open to a vast public audience and reflecting the democratising trends of the Revolution. It was the city of Paris itself. Over the course of the nineteenth century and reappearing in the late twentieth century, public officials turned the city into a display of technological innovations that served as a means of public education. A succession of national governments from the First to the Fifth Republics encouraged these innovations and engineered the cityscape, in part because they saw this man-made environment as a powerful vehicle for political reform and social control, as well as a field for economic development. Urban technological display offered an attractive alternative to overt coercion as a means of realising these goals.[2]

There was also a potential audience for these displays. Crowds of working-class people hopeful and discontent, were a hallmark of Paris from the Revolution on. The authorities wished both to keep them under control and to direct their energies into useful activity.[3] In addition, the intense focus on life in the public sphere at that time, followed by the revival of commercial activity beginning in the 1820s and 1830s, drew the lower middle classes and the bourgeoisie outside their neighbourhoods, curious to see the passing scene and anxious to be seen by those passing by. The mid-nineteenth century brought a new figure into the urban scene: the *flaneur*, an individual who strolled through the streets, seeking to equilibrate himself through visual intercourse with the ever-changing urban panorama. In Charles Baudelaire's view, he "... sought to become one flesh with the crowd. For the perfect *flaneur*, for the passionate spectator, it is an immense joy to set up house in the heart of the multitude, amid the ebb and flow of movement, in the midst of the fugitive and the infinite." [4]

In the later nineteenth century, the liberalisation of political and economic life under the Third Republic brought large numbers of middle-class people out into public spaces to spend their leisure time in a variety of new commercial pastimes, including going to cafés, the popular theatre and amusement parks.[5] If the authorities had urban technological displays to offer over the course of the century, they had several audiences primed to be responsive to the messages conveyed.

In the following discussion, a brief history of the use of Paris as a museum of technology will be presented, paying special attention to two projects of a group of Republican reformers in the Third Republic: the universal exposition of 1889 and the decoration of the streets with posters advertising new technologies. The last decades of the nineteenth century constitute a transition period in this instrumental approach to the city. The commercial success of the exposition and the posters led supporters to recognise the benefits of a formal institutional structure — a museum in the more conventional sense of the term. A building housing a collection of technological artifacts promised a controlled environment designed to emphasise the moral and social implications of technological experience, as distinct, but not totally divorced, from its value in the market-place. Such a building would have its heirs in the Centre Pompidou and the Cité des Sciences et de l'Industrie at La Villette.

The first conscious use of Paris in this way was the revolutionary festival of the Supreme Being held in August of 1794. Masses of new citizens participated in a public event celebrating the Republic's commitment to social progress based on the exercise of liberty, equality, fraternity and industry.[6] A series of pyrotechnic displays associated with the image of justice marked the path participants followed from their homes in the manufacturing and commercial quarters across the length of the city. Arriving at the Champ de Mars on the eastern edge, they encircled a huge artificial mountain built for the occasion, dedicating themselves to promote the welfare of the nation. This event was followed four years later by a festive public parade of French manufacturers and inventors through the city to the Champ de Mars where the first national exposition of French industry and arts was housed.[7]

In the years of the Restoration and July Monarchy (1815-1848) more permanent displays of technology were introduced. Among the most important were the construction of twenty-nine innovatively designed iron and glass arcades and passages housing commercial businesses. They were a popular novelty, drawing the public in off the damp streets and encouraging them to browse and buy at their leisure in naturally lit, sheltered comfort.[8]

The extensive rebuilding of Paris in the 1850s was a more ambitious effort to institute social control, which came on the heels of the 1848 uprisings. Baron Haussmann, who directed the project during the Second Empire, made use of new technologies, building materials and design concepts to produce an integrated urban system. Haussmann also turned large parts of the city into parks simulating country estates in which artifice was unabashedly used to mimic nature. In them, the public enjoyed the view from atop artificial rock outcroppings constructed from concrete and strolled on grassy slopes enclosed with miles of mass-produced fencing cast in the shape of tree branches.[9] According to a report to the Municipal Commission on the value of rebuilding Paris, the administration used various technologies and techniques to "... assure the public tranquility by the creation of grands boulevards which allow for the circulation of air and light, as well as troops, and through an ingenious combination, render the people better behaved and less disposed to revolt".[10]

This effort at social control was modified with the advent of Republican ministers to office in the 1880s. They sought to reform what they viewed as a repressive and dishonest moral environment by changing the physical appearance of the entire urban setting. These new men found the walls of Haussmann's city grey and comfortless. Emile Zola felt the geometric plan of the cemetery on the city's edge and the railroad that ringed it to be bureaucratic tools for levering the poor into social anonymity.[11] Reformers called for a more aesthetically honest and economically varied urban setting as a means of encouraging every person to seek personal enjoyment on their own initiative. As a corrective they sought to turn the entire city of Paris into a technological museum devoted to liberal democratic ends.[12]

In effect, the idea of using the city as a museum of technology came of age at the moment when the government of the Third Republic sought to mount a major international exposition of arts and industries on the Champ de Mars and to decorate urban spaces with coloured posters advertising new consumer technologies. Each of the projects altered the cityscape, but in different ways. Both were enormously popular, but the goals of each were compromised by the domination of commercial interests, which had been under governmental control in earlier regimes. Commercial competition created a kind of social entropy which made it clear that urban spaces were now partially in the hands of new interest groups. The Republican government found an alternative in the creation of more conventional forms of museums which retained a link with the earlier commitments to technological display as a means of public education.

The exposition of 1889 was originally intended to celebrate the centenary of the inauguration of freedom to work established by the Revolution. It spanned hundreds of acres on the Champ de Mars, along the Seine and across the bridge over the river onto the hill of the Trocadero. Ambitiously large and innovatively designed buildings allowed millions of French citizens to view the achievements of French industry operating in a Republican system. The educational character of the exposition was apparent in the numerous displays which manufacturers such as Thomas Edison had mounted to show how their new machines worked. It was also evident in the unadorned character of buildings such as the *galerie des machines* and the Eiffel Tower, which served as a gateway to the exposition.
Their structural skeletons were laid bare to reveal elegant and easily grasped solutions to problems of bridging great spaces and reaching great heights. One of the exposition's major political supporters, the Minister Edouard Lockroy, waxed poetic in his celebration of the Eiffel Tower as a symbol of progress which drew all those who climbed it together into a futuristic experience of utopian community.[13]

Yet Lockroy was disappointed in the exposition because it had become too commercialised. It had lost the dignity appropriate to a national festival when a new administration allowed cafés, popular entertainments, restaurants, souvenir sellers and a host of street vendors access to the fair. In the end it had become a huge market which threatened to become a permanent fixture. To this Lockroy responded with the argument that industrial expositions were sacred civic events to be held periodically so that the citizens could take a measure of their common achievements and be inspired to work together to excel themselves. At these times, commercial interests had to be held subordinate to the goals of social solidarity and the public good.

The program for posters was no less popular than that for the exposition, and no more able to prevent the influx of commercial interests. In the mid-1880s at the time the exposition was being planned, a movement had been launched to bring together the talents, skills and technologies of small-scale producers in the printing trades with those of artists and publishers. Promoters, among them Edouard Lockroy, Ernest Maindron, André Mellerio and Roger Marx, aimed to use colour illustrated posters to give a new face to the Parisian cityscape, in the process of being rebuilt after the destruction of the Franco-Prussian War and the Commune. In so doing, they hoped to bring the economically and physically segregated populations of the city together through participation in a common aesthetic experience.

The city offered in fact, a perfect physical space for the display of these images. It was not simply a matter of mitigating the harsh character of the industrial landscape, but of replacing that vista with an entirely new panorama tailored to their definition of the sensibilities of the ordinary passer-by. The surroundings would be entirely congenial to individual sensibilities and at the same time democratic because the experience was accessible to everyone at any number of places for free. Ernest Maindron, the government official who organised a series of exhibitions on the poster and authored two books on the subject, found posters created a new environment, becoming part of an altered condition of existence, where people and poster images seemed part of the same democratic reality. In 1886 Maindron enthusiastically described the effect which posters had on the ambiance of public spaces. "A person has only

M. R. LEVIN

Fig.1 Eiffel Tower and Construction of the Fountain of Progress, artist unknown, 1889. (Courtesy of the Library of Congress, Washington, D.C.)

to experience the charm of the vision that is interjected into his path", he wrote, to realise how posters transformed the character of the street for the better. He compared the street to an open air museum where the poster found its *raison d'être*. It was, he said, "always animated, in motion, a place where universal suffrage was discussed and acclaimed".[14]

In Maindron's view, the colourful advertisements acted as a natural catalyst for innate political energies and aspirations that lay dormant within the population. The arrangement of large sheets of paper on the walls gave order and meaning to the vistas that met people's gaze without being coercive. In fact, he finds the spirit and rhythms of the poster-lined spaces and of the people within them blend together in a perfect harmony. Ten years later he would look back on this early period and feel that some of the promises of these visions had been realised. "It was a great joy for [the people] to note that barren factory walls and the cold and naked palisades of buildings under construction had become veritable museums where the masses, reflective and attracted to art, now find some of their aspirations satisfied. This type of education was made to seduce the crowd: they see quite well that the street which they love in order to please them has made herself more colourful, more sparkling than she had ever been".[15]

Yet, it is important to note the promise which posters fulfilled, as he saw it, was that of creating a population that was more subdued and conscious of personal feelings. There was now a large group of individuals increasingly responsive to the pleasures which certain forms of aesthetic experience provided them. The colour and variety had been used to woo and marry them to the new liberal democratic order.

The young critic André Mellerio took up the same line of reasoning as he pointed out the role which artists and printers had played in creating this new aesthetic ambiance. Citing the works of the prolific poster artist Jules Chéret, he called them, "the frescoes, if not of the poor, at least of the crowd." Raising the question of what role the poster could play in the present social order, he responded " [posters could put] the public in touch with its everyday feelings."[16]

Promoters argued that the artist more than any other person was responsible for manipulating the technology so that the poster produced this effect. In particular it was this individual, described as a skilled and imaginative worker, who was best able to master and exploit the process. Mellerio pointed out that the colour lithographic process, although not entirely new in the early 1880s, was "given a large and resounding influence" through the efforts of artist-printers like Jules Chéret, who took a "simple sheet of paper for which mechanical means procured the advantage of unlimited copies." In addition to extending the influence of these images through replication, supporters attributed the success of this means of communication to the new conditions of production that favoured the small craft producer. Poster artists worked closely and easily with printers in intimate settings using hand-operated presses. The shop of the printer Clôt was "a friendly place... in comparison with big printing factories, which impose themselves in an overwhelming fashion...".[17]

The number of posters produced is not known, but was significant. For example, Steinlein between 1891 and 1900 made over thirty-six large posters, most of them with figures drawn to life-size; however, the posters themselves often expressed certain witty permutations on the theme of the liberating and community-forming effect they were assumed to have. Advertisements for bicycles often emphasised these feelings. An iconography of liberty developed centred in images of women on bicycles. In a poster by Albert Guillaume for Peugeot products, the artist expresses the social bonding effect produced among men of different social ranks and ages by an advertisement for the Paris-Nantes bicycle race. As viewers of this poster, we too participate in the process of community building through the shared experience of looking at posters. Another work commissioned from the prolific poster artist Steinlein is a *tour de force* of five colours. Its subject is the very ambience of democratized society created by posters. Working people and members of the bourgeoisie are shown gathered together watching the poster hanger

Fig. 2 "La Galerie des Machines", from *La revue illustrée, 1889*. (Courtesy of the Library of Congress, Washington, D.C.)

mount an advertisement for an international industrial exposition in Madrid. At the time of their first appearance in large numbers, then, posters were the product of a small-scale technology whose display was thought capable of bringing to prominence a large and previously unrepresented segment of French society. One set of beneficiaries was the middle and working classes, the newly enfranchised populations of the Third Republic. The large images pasted up side by side, appearing repeatedly in public places throughout the city, created for them a seemingly free space where they escaped the confines of modern industrial life. Users of the presses whose products had become so popular also stood to gain. Printers, artists and publishers working together in small print shops would make a place for themselves in the newly liberalised marketplace of the late 1880s.

Despite such success in the middle and late 1890s, we find the writers who once enthusiastically supported the poster expressing their doubts. On the one hand, a critic complained that these advertisements misrepresented the product advertised. Maindron admitted that he preferred the beauty of a poster promoting the bicycle to the actual pain of learning to ride the vehicle. More disappointing was the realisation that posters were ephemeral products. Roger Marx likened the walls covered with posters to a fairy garden in which flowers bloomed magnificently and then faded in the sun and rain. Their effect was transitory and required continuous renewal.[18]

All three men also felt that contrary to their expectations for the community-forming mystique of posters produced by these small groups of craftsmen, the liberalisation of French society had permitted a new stressful and alienating situation to develop. Circumstances had encouraged middle-men to treat lithographed posters as a source of ever-renewable profits because they had become consumer goods subject to the market forces of supply and demand.

These discoveries where accompanied by a growing antipathy in attitudes towards the public spaces themselves. Beginning in 1896, Roger Marx found it a trying experience to pass through these spaces decorated with posters. He complained that the very walls conspired against giving the gaze of passers-by any rest. By 1900 he had retreated from the street and was urging artists to cooperate in the production of limited editions of colour lithographs for middle-class domestic interiors. Most significantly, Maindron was advocating that examples of the best

Fig. 3 Exposition de Madrid. Théophile-Alexandre Steinlein, 1893.

posters be preserved in a special museum, a formal enclosed space set aside for that purpose, where colour lithographed advertisements could be housed and exhibited out of reach of commercial influences. Instead they would serve as documents of a period when the technology of colour lithography flourished.[19]

Although these reformers retreated from advocating the display of lithographed posters on city walls as a democratising form of technological culture, the idea of the city as a museum of technology serving social and economic ends was not abandoned. In the twentieth century in Paris we find that the original idea has been refined and adapted, while the goal of serving the interests of democracy in the sense of reaching all social classes and providing a common ground for understanding, has proved useful in a revised form. Even the metal and glass structures and bright primary colours that had characterised the nineteenth-century vision of democratic technology offered a precedent, if not a model, for a new museum architecture.[20]

Supporters of the Beaubourg, planned in the decade after the popular demonstrations and

Fig. 4 *Cité des Sciences et de l'Industrie.* Pierre Carrère, 1991. (Courtesy of P. Carrère / Cité des Sciences et de l'Industrie)

confrontations of May 1968, proposed the building as a museum that would bring high art to the people. In its exterior design, its siting, the organisation of its interior spaces and even in the art it displays, the Beaubourg reveals itself as an heir to these nineteenth-century concepts of the city as a museum of technology. It has served to canalise the attention and to integrate diverse populations without being overtly oppressive.

The architecture of the Beaubourg, which seems so radical at close-hand, finds a certain aesthetic and technological fit with other older structures in this part of the city: the iron and glass dome of the Bourse de Commerce of 1801 and the Gothic structure of the nearby Church of St. Merri. It is also reminiscent of those arcades and exposition buildings of the earlier era. The siting of the Beaubourg successfully invites a gathering of the public around it. Bright primary colours proclaim it a place where there are pleasures for all ages. Free admission, transparent glass walls and escalator tubes encourage people to enter and freely explore the interior spaces as simple extensions of the outside space. The interior spaces are divided in a seemingly casual way between free services (library) and exhibits (the design centre) and special exhibitions for which one pays admission. One, therefore, is engaged immediately in making choices, interacting with the environment to find one's way, and various exhibits often rely on hands-on experience with computers and other technologies. Much of the art and industrial design is directly related to the adaptation of new technologies into modern life.[21]

Yet, despite this openness and integration on a technological level, the techniques of organisation and display at the Beaubourg have created diverse audiences, and there is little interest in it on the part of the working classes (blue-collar workers and their families), according to studies done by the administration. It is rather the upper middle classes and street people, as well as students who utilise it. Those who work with their hands and with machines for a living prefer other forms of leisure activity.[22]

Much the same is true for La Villette's design and for the audiences it draws. Thus, if we recognise that any claims of reaching all citizens and profoundly shaping their consciousness are hopelessly utopian and happily unrealisable, yet socially and economically useful goals, we may see that La Villette is a museum which can be considered a city of technology in itself. It is an environment openly recognised by its planners as partly an instrument of commercial development for the city, as well as a national institution for promoting science and technology. The imaginative character of its exhibits, its spatial arrangements and interior and exterior design offer the possibility of achieving its enlightened goal of educating those sectors of the population who are increasingly separated from creative scientific and technological activity in their daily lives.

What remains to be seen, but is not impossible, is that such a museum can serve among policy-makers and informed citizens to increase curiosity and critical consideration of the uses to which science and technology are being put in contemporary society. One hopeful example is the large exhibition on water which is being accompanied by conferences for the public and by seminars where scientists, engineers and administrators consider problems of distribution and conservation.[23] In this way the two educational functions of the museum inaugurated in the Revolution may be joined in one institution. Whether such a museum can take a critical view, as well as offer a progressive vision of technology remains to be seen. This is the new challenge for public museum education in the twenty-first century.

Notes

1 Alexandre Herlea, "Advanced Technology Education and Industrial Research Laboratories in 19th Century France: The Example of Conservatoire des arts et métiers in Paris," in Melvin Kranzberg (ed.), *Technological Education - Technological Style*. San Francisco, San Francisco Press, 1986, pp. 49-57.
2 See the discussion of Foucault in David Harvey, *The Condition of Post Modernity*. Oxford, Basil Blackwell, 1989, pp. 44-46. Harvey introduces economics into Foucault's equation of power relationships.
3 For history of crowds in France see the classic work by Georges Rudé, *The Crowd in History: A Study of Popular Disturbances in France and England, 1730-1848*. London, Lawrence and Wishart, 1981.
4 Charles Baudelaire, *The Painter of Modern Life and Other Essays*, trans. by Jonathan Mayne. New York, Phaidon, 1964, p. 9.
5 *Ibid*. See also Susanna Barrows, *Distorting Mirrors: Vision of the Crowd in Late Nineteenth Century France*. New Haven, Yale University Press, 1981. The subject of the public sphere has been a topic much discussed by American historians of the French Revolution in recent years. It has centred around the concept of the public sphere introduced by Jürgen Habermas in *Der philosophische Diskurs der Moderne*.
6 William Sewell, *Work and Revolution in France: The Language of Labor from the Old Regime to 1848*. Cambridge-New York, Cambridge University Press, 1980.
7 Ernest Maindron, *Le Champ de Mars, 1751-1889*. Paris, 1889; Miriam R. Levin, "The Wedding of Art and Science in Late Eighteenth Century France", *Eighteenth Century Life* (May 1982), pp. 54-73; Miriam Levin, *Republican Art and Ideology in Late Nineteenth Century France*. Ann Arbor, UMI Press, 1986, pp. 107-8 and figures 9 and 10; Daryl Hafter, "The Business of Invention in the Paris Industrial Exposition of 1806", *Business History Review* 58 (Autumn 1984), p. 319; Mona Ozouf, *Fête révolutionnaire, 1789-1799*. Paris, 1976.
8 See Paul Chemetov, *Familièrement inconnu: Architectures, Paris 1848-1914*. Paris, C.N.M.H.S., 1972, pp. 14-16; Susan Buck-Morse, *The Dialectics of Seeing: Walter Benjamin and the Arcades Project*. Cambridge, MA, M.I.T. Press, 1989.
9 David Pinkney, *Napoleon III and the Rebuilding of Paris*. Princeton, Princeton University Press, 1958; Bonnie Grad and Timothy Riggs, *Vision of City and Country: Prints and Photographs of Nineteenth Century France*. Worcester, MA, Worcester Art Museum, 1982, pp. 192 and 204.
10 *Ibid.*, p. 192.
11 Huysmans, "Chéret", *Certains*, Paris, 1882 (?), p. 52.
12 M.R. Levin, *Republican Art and Ideology, op.cit.*, 1986.
13 Edouard Lockroy, "Preface," in Emile Monod (ed.), *L'Exposition universelle de 1889*. Paris, E. Dentu, 1890, vol. 1, p. XVII.
14 *Les Affiches illustrées*. Paris, 1886, pp. I-II.

15 *Ibid.*, p. 2.
16 *La Lithographie originale en couleurs.* Paris, L'Estampe et l'affiche, 1898, translated and reprinted in Phillip Dennis Cate and Sinclair Hitchings, *The Color Revolution: Color Lithography in France 1890-1900.* Santa Barbara and Salt Lake City, 1978, pp. 28-29 and 95.
17 *Ibid.*, pp. 80 and 91.
18 E. Maindron, *Les Affiches, op.cit.*, 1886-1895, p. 119; Roger Marx, *Les Maîtres de l'affiche.* Vol.I, 1896, p. III.
19 *Ibid.*, vol. I, 1896, p. III, and vol. V, 1900, pp. I-IV.
20 Natalie Heinich, "The Pompidou Centre and Its Public: The Limits of a Utopian Site", (trans. by Chris Turner) in Robert Lumley (ed.), *The Museum Time Machine.* New York, Routledge, 1988, pp. 199-212.
21 *Ibid.* Also see brochure published by Connaissance des Arts titled *Le Centre Georges Pompidou,* n.d.
22 See N. Heinich, *loc.cit.*
23 See for example Kenneth Hudson, *Museums of Influence.* Cambridge, Cambridge University Press, 1987, section on present and future oriented centres; David Douglas, *The Museum Transformed: Design and Culture in the Post-Pompidou Age.* New York, Abbeville, 1990; Alan Morton, "Science Museums and the Future" in R. Lumley (ed.), *The Museum Time Machine, op.cit.*, pp. 140-141, discusses the way in which the display of objects in context of "progress" puts them out of context of human use. Only the most perfect solutions are shown.

AN OLYMPIC STADIUM OF TECHNOLOGY:
Deutsches Museum and Sweden's Tekniska Museet

Svante Lindqvist

Royal Institute of Technology, Stockholm, Sweden

Introduction

For many years, I had the privilege of being a pupil of Torsten Althin (1897-1982).[1] He had been director of Sweden's Tekniska Museet for thirty-eight years (1924-1962), and was now teaching history of technology at the Royal Institute of Technology, the engineering school in Stockholm. On formal occasions, Althin always wore the *goldenen Ehrenring des Deutschen Museums*, a thick, heavy ring in solid gold bearing the symbolic owl of the Deutsches Museum. He used to hum arias from *Die Meistersinger*, and he would often speak of the time when he saw Richard Strauss conduct. We shared a small office in the Royal Institute of Technology, and from the window we could see the nearby towers of the red-brick stadium that had been built for the Olympic Games in Stockholm in 1912. When Torsten Althin received the Leonardo da Vinci Medal from the Society for the History of Technology in 1978, he proudly pointed out that he had received his first medal in that very stadium in 1912.[2] It had been a memorial medal given to each of the many hundreds of boy scouts who served as messengers during the Fifth Olympiad in Stockholm. Young Torsten's particular assignment had been to put the big brass numerals up on the boards that announced the results to the public.

Torsten Althin was then in his early eighties and something of a legend in the Swedish museum world. He was also well-known to several generations of Swedish engineers, and he had often known the grandfathers as well as the fathers of the engineering students who now filled the lecture hall. Ten or fifteen years earlier, in the early 1960s, he had been at the peak of his reputation in the international museum world, but he had by now outlived most of his many friends in I.C.O.M. and the museums of postwar Europe and the United States. He maintained, however, a lively correspondence with historians of technology abroad.[3] He received a constant stream of visitors in our little office, enthusiastically sharing with them his encyclopaedic knowledge and many anecdotes of the past.

Ten years after his death, the memory of this elderly man at his desk, chain-smoking and talking incessantly, has taken on a new significance for me. The retired director of Tekniska Museet, reminiscing about Munich in the 1920s and the Olympic Games in Stockholm in 1912, represented an interesting development in the history of technical museums. This development is, however, not only of interest from a Swedish point of view but also illustrative of some of the general problems facing museums of technology.[4]

The Nationalistic Heritage: International Exhibitions and Olympic Games

The Deutsches Museum in Munich was established in 1903, but due to the war the museum building was not finished until 1925.[5] Although the museum was situated in the capital of

Bavaria, it was considered a pan-German museum. The ability to complete this huge museum according to plan during the difficult years of the recession in the early 1920s was a sign to Germany — and to the rest of the world — that the nation had recovered from war. The consecration was a combination of a Bavarian *fête* with street parades and a more solemn state occasion with a huge formal opening ceremony followed by a gala performance at the opera.

After the opening of the Deutsches Museum in 1925 there were enthusiastic reports in the Swedish daily press of this new and incredible museum. But only a year later, critical voices were raised. One newspaper devoted a whole page to an article with the headline "Sweden badly represented at the Deutsches Museum", and the subtitle "The Royal Swedish Academy of Engineering Sciences is watching the situation".[6] The article contained a survey of the museum — department by department — and for almost every department there was a Swede with an invention who the paper thought should have been represented by an artifact or at least mentioned. Another newspaper made a similar survey of Sweden in the Deutsches Museum under the heading "Meagerly represented, sometimes with no labels of nationality".[7] The article claimed that the only object in the Deutsches Museum that originated from Sweden was a pair of shoes from Lapland.

Why had Swedish engineers and their inventions not received the recognition that Swedish critics in 1926 thought they deserved? It was suggested in one of the articles that "we Swedes are too modest, too reluctant to blow our own trumpet", and that this was why Swedish engineers were unknown abroad.[8] However, Conrad Matschoss' biographical dictionary, *Männer der Technik*, published by the Verein Deutscher Ingenieure in 1925, contains entries for all Swedish engineers who might be expected to be included in a limited, international selection such as this.[9] For example, the biography of the Swedish eighteenth century inventor

Fig. 1 From the opening ceremony of the Olympic Games in Stockholm in 1912. The different national teams parade in the stadium and salute the King of Sweden on the royal stand. (Photo *Kungliga biblioteket*, Stockholm)

Christopher Polhem is substantial and in all respects correct. Swedish engineers were thus not unknown abroad, and definitely not in Germany in 1925, but the Swedish criticism of the Deutsches Museum is interesting because it tells us how the role of a technical museum was perceived in Sweden at the time. We Swedes had not grasped the fact that the aim of the Deutsches Museum was to show the main stages of the international development of technology. In fact, in Sweden museums of technology were seen in rather the same way as the international exhibitions of the nineteenth century. In an article in *Technology and Culture* in 1965, Eugene S. Ferguson showed that it was from these exhibitions that the modern museums of technology to some extent grew.[10] An important aspect of the international exhibitions was national rivalry. They have often been described as "arenas of peaceful competition between the nations", but national rivalry it nevertheless was. International competitions in military strength are, of course, as old as society itself, but the idea of formal, non-military, international competitions is relatively recent — an innovation of the industrial society. The international exhibitions of the nineteenth century may be regarded as an early institutionalisation of this idea. The industrial products were grouped in different classes, the winners of each class awarded gold medals and the nations ranked accordingly in the reports of the judges. This was how Swedish visitors in the 1920s viewed the Deutsches Museum: as an international exhibition with a temporal dimension. When they passed through the halls and galleries of the Deutsches Museum, it was to see whether Sweden had been awarded the gold medals that were our due in the various classes.

To this another contemporary tradition can be added that may have helped to provoke Swedish criticism. A second and somewhat later form of formal competition for the sake of national prestige was the Olympic Games, which were institutionalised in the late nineteenth century. The athletic games of Ancient Greece, we are told, were "revived" during the 1880s, and the first modern Olympic Games were held in Athens in 1896 "as a token of respect to their origin". However, this symbolic gesture should not lead us to misinterpret the Olympic Games as anything but another expression of international competition in industrial society.[11] It is noteworthy that the second Olympic Games were held during the Paris Exposition of 1900, and that the third took place at the St. Louis World's Fair of 1904 — i.e., they were held in conjunction with the two major international exhibitions at the turn of the century.

Later, the international exhibitions and the Olympic Games went their separate ways — in location as well as in importance. The role of the international exhibitions diminished rapidly during the first half of the twentieth century, and their practical function for trade and technology diffusion had by the middle of the century been taken over by industrial fairs for specific branches.[12] The significance of the Olympic Games, however, increased and eventually took over the role of the international exhibitions as arenas for symbolic non-military national competition. As the twentieth century has progressed, it has become more and more obvious that the Olympic Games are just another yardstick of the relative economic strength of the industrialised nations, they are "forums for international competition and are utilised as tools of national foreign policy".[13] In the Olympic Games, nations competed in various classes as they had done in the international exhibitions. Here, too, the winners were awarded gold medals by impartial referees, the number of national medals totalled and the nations ranked accordingly.

The juries' reports of the international exhibitions had been published in large, heavy volumes, which were often translated into other languages and distributed widely. Very similar to these symbols of national prestige is the 1,117-page, richly illustrated *Official Report on the Olympic Games of Stockholm 1912*.[14] Although the Fifth Olympiad in Stockholm was unusually large, with three thousand competitors from twenty-eight nations, we stand in awe at the interest that must have been aroused before a Swedish publisher could be commissioned to undertake such a huge, international project.[15] The solemn faces of the athletes, posing in national teams before the photographers in Stockholm 1912, conveys the contemporary importance and the national rivalry of these competitions. The teams members of the various equestrian sports were all officers in uniform, and it almost seems as if the Fifth Olympiad in Stockholm 1912 was a dress-rehearsal for the First World War.

The Olympic Games were resumed in Antwerp in 1920 in a war-torn Belgium. In their capacity as official losers of the war, Germany and Austria had been forbidden to participate by the International Olympic Committee; Russia was in a turmoil and did not take part either. The following Olympiad, Paris 1924, was the largest so far, but Germany — which had by then been forgiven by the I.O.C. — chose to sulk and did not participate. The significance of the Deutsches Museum in 1925 should be seen in this perspective, and this also allows us to understand the reaction of the Swedish visitors more thoroughly. The idea of formal international competition was thus very much alive at the time of the opening of the museum, and the Swedish visitors looked on the Deutsches Museum as an Olympic stadium of technology. They were vexed at the decision of the invisible umpires, and considered Sweden unjustly marked.

A Role for History in the Professionalisation of Engineers

Among the invited speakers at the opening ceremony of the Deutsches Museum in 1925 was a Swede, the renowned Asian explorer and fanatical pro-German Sven Hedin (1865-1952). His speech in Munich was reported by many Swedish daily papers, which noted proudly that it had received an ovation.[16] But among the invited guests at the opening ceremony there was another Swede: Torsten Althin, the young curator of Sweden's Tekniska Museet, which had been established only a year before. Althin noted proudly in his travel diary that he had met Oskar von Miller (1855-1934), the legendary director of the Deutsches Museum, on both the 6th and 8th of May, and that he had spent much of his time in the company of the conductor and composer Richard Strauss (1864-1949).[17]

The idea of a Swedish museum of technology was inspired by the example of the Deutsches Museum. The building of such a museum was first suggested in 1910 by a Swedish engineer who had visited the temporary exhibition halls of the Deutsches Museum in Munich. He presented his idea at a talk to the Swedish Society of Graduate Engineers (Svenska Teknologföreningen), which was then starting to make plans for its fiftieth anniversary in the following year.[18] The jubilee of 1911 was an important occasion for the society. The Swedish engineers faced, as Bo Sundin has shown, their own peculiar problems at the beginning of the twentieth century.[19] Sweden had been industrialised late by comparison with other European countries, and the corps of engineers that had emerged during the latter half of the nineteenth century had difficulty in gaining acceptance and recognition in a nation which was by and large still an agrarian society governed by an established upper class of civil servants educated in the classics and trained in law. For the jubilee in 1911, the Swedish engineering community searched for symbols that could demonstrate the long tradition of the young profession and its importance to the development of the nation.

A Swedish museum of technology could be such a symbol, but it was to be another twenty-five years before this idea was realised.[20] Instead, another, less cumbersome symbol for the jubilee was chosen, after it was noticed that the year 1911 coincided with the 250th anniversary of the birth of Christopher Polhem (1661-1751), the famous eighteenth-century Swedish inventor. The society appointed an editorial committee to produce a *Festschrift* on Polhem which was duly published in 1911.[21] This book became highly influential in shaping the image of Christopher Polhem. The history of his life was dramatised in numerous popular accounts, becoming a recurrent topic for talks on the radio, features in magazines and popular lectures. He became our own Thomas Edison, our own James Watt.

In the early twentieth century, Swedish engineers, according to Sundin, faced a dilemma. They had gained a grudging and precarious position in the upper strata of society by referring to the scientific component of engineering. By claiming that their work was based upon scientific principles they were able to draw on the social prestige that the cultural phenomenon of science and its practitioners have enjoyed in Western society since the late seventeenth century. This, however, carried little weight with Swedish industry, which by this time was facing the problems of structural change implied by the development of large-scale processes and technological systems, as well as the growing demand for rationalisation. What were the engineers to do? If they responded to the demands of industry they would lose the status they had gained. If, on the other hand, they stuck to their claim that engineering was applied basic science they would lose the support of industry. In this situation, Sundin writes, they came upon a brilliant solution. They coined a new Swedish word "*ingenjörsvetenskap*", engineering science, as a branch of knowledge in its own right: epistemologically distinct from science as well as from economics, but yet including elements from both. The symbol of this social invention was the founding of a new royal academy: Ingenjörsvetenskapsakademien (the Royal Swedish Academy of Engineering Sciences).

The academy, founded in 1919, became the first engineering academy in the world. But the Swedish engineers also needed a less sophisticated symbol to gain social recognition and to win acceptance of their professional claims in the eyes of the general public. A museum, as mentioned above, had been discussed earlier as a means of gaining respect as a professional group by referring to important predecessors and to a long professional tradition. The new academy became an institution that was strong enough to carry out such a project, and a Swedish museum of technology, Tekniska Museet, was founded in 1924. The president of the academy, Axel F. Enström (1875-1948), began to look for a suitable candidate to take charge of the museum, as yet non-existant. He found such a person in Torsten Althin at the Gothenburg Jubilee Exhibition of 1923.

Artifacts and the Technological Enthusiasm of the 1920s

Torsten Althin grew up in a rectory in a village in the province of Scania in southern Sweden, where his father was the seventh in a line of priests in the Lutheran church.[22] His father was interested in music, and translated Wagner librettos into Swedish in his spare time. On stormy nights, when his children woke up afraid of the thunder and lightning, he used to gather them in the dark living room and play Wagner on the piano "to calm them down" as the rain was beating against the window-panes — a childhood experience most of us are fortunate to have escaped.[23] Scania, like most parts of Sweden at the time, was a sparsely populated rural area. The milk separator, the Mauser rifle and the traction engine were probably the only products of the new industrialised world that had reached the parish by the turn of the century. Torsten Althin often related that he did not see his first car until he visited Stockholm in 1906. He also spoke of the excitement when one day a man walked into the village with a wooden box on his back, containing a strange-looking machine. After the sun had set, the man nailed a sheet to a barn-door and showed the astounded villagers (including the curate's son) the first motion pictures any of them had seen. Torsten Althin later claimed that he wanted to become an engineer, but that the First World War changed his plans.[24] This may sound plausible, but Sweden was never affected by the war. It is more likely that his father could not afford to send him to university, but that Althin wanted to break away from his Wagnerian father (who had remarried after the death of his first wife). Be that as it may, after graduating from the Gymnasium in Ystad in 1915, Althin embarked on a military career and received his commission in 1917 in a mounted artillery regiment, Kungl. Wendes Artilleriregemente, stationed in the nearby town of Kristianstad. The First World War saw many new technological innovations of military warfare, and we must remember how drastic these changes were. The mounted artillery in southern Sweden, for example, had been trained to meet the unlikely event of an enemy invading the plains of Scania using the techniques and equipment of the Franco-German war, but now the regiment was facing new technologies. Althin once told me how the regiment prepared itself to meet the new threat of the aeroplane: the wheels of a howitzer were nailed to a huge barn door that had been unhinged and laid on the ground. A pilot in one of the few Swedish biplanes available at the time flew back and forth over the artillery range with an empty beet sack hanging behind the plane on a long rope. With their combined strength, the gun crew were able to lift one end of the barn door and turn the howitzer in the direction of the target — the beet sack — moving rapidly across the sky behind the brave pilot.

The fact that we find this story about early anti-aircraft defence quaint, even amusing, illustrates the general difficulty of appreciating how earlier generations tried to come to grips with technological innovations. Future generations will, of course, find our own attempts just as amusing. For example, the advice to civilians after the Second World War to wear sunglasses and remain indoors in case of a nuclear war has already begun to appear similarly picturesque in its inadequacy. However, the use of a barn door, a rope and an empty beet sack made some sense in rural Scania, and it showed an ability to adapt to a new technological situation that had suddenly made warfare three-dimensional. It should not be measured by the standards of our own time, the era of Scud missiles and Patriot robots.

The point here, however, is that this episode illustrates a qualitative difference between our own perception of technological change and that which prevailed in the 1920s. The First World War brought many new technologies to the civilian life of the interwar period, and Western society experienced a feeling of tremendous technological advancement. The war was seen as a watershed between the modern industrialised world and the old agrarian society. Such technical novelties as radios, aeroplanes, Zeppelins, motion pictures and automobiles had all existed before the war, but it was during the 1920s that they became, if not within the reach of the man in the street, at least part of the common technological world. These changes were probably as dramatic as anything we have experienced since the Second World War. This, too, was a feeling that sought its expression in museums of technology in the 1920s. But it was a technological enthusiasm that fed on new *artifacts* rather than on new systems or new concepts.[25] The technological enthusiasm of the late nineteenth century had been based on new *systems* such as electric power and lighting, railways, telegraphs and telephones. The technological enthusiasm of our own time — permanent as it seems to be in industrial society, despite all undercurrents of criticism — is based on such new *concepts* as information technology and bioengineering. The artifact-oriented technological enthusiasm of the 1920s was of relevance for one of the more crucial conceptual choices of the Swedish museum.

In 1920, when wondering how a young subaltern could afford to get married on his salary, Torsten Althin saw a newspaper advertisement seeking a "young, culturally interested officer for administrative work with good prospects".[26] The advertisement had been placed by Sigurd Erixon (1888-1968), curator at the Nordic Museum in Stockholm and later the first Swedish professor in Nordic and Comparative Ethnology. He was in charge of planning the historical section of the Tricentennial Exhibition of the City of Gothenburg, and he was now looking for someone who could collect objects, tools and machinery for a display on the history of Swedish industry.

Althin's formal museum education was surprisingly short for someone who was to make such a remarkable career in the museum world. Time was of the essence in getting the Gothenburg exhibition ready for the tricentennial year, and Althin was given a two-week course in museology at the Nordic Museum. He spent this time learning how to handle a huge wooden

camera with its fragile glass plates, and how to write object cards in script.[27] His training completed
— which must have been quite a change from commanding artillery troopers — Althin began
the first Swedish collection devoted to industrial history.

In Sweden in the 1920s, the old pre-industrial society still lived side by side with the
emerging industrial nation. In the mining districts, the blast furnaces were still fired with
charcoal and the squeak of *Stangenkunsts* could still be heard as they transmitted the power
from the waterwheels through their connected wooden beams to the bellows and tilt-hammers
in the forges. In a textile mill in southern Sweden, Althin found an eighteenth-century
"Spinning Jenny", still in daily use. But he not only collected artifacts and archival material,
he was also the first in Sweden to document old industrial processes and working conditions
on cine-film.

The Gothenburg Exhibition in 1923 was an innovative departure from the Swedish museum
tradition as it portended the *Functionalist* movement traditionally associated with the
Stockholm Exhibition of 1930. But the exhibition turned out to be, in Torsten Althin's own
words, "a tremendous financial fiasco".[28] The collection of objects in the display of industrial
history was stored for an unknown future,[29] and it was at this point that Althin came to the notice
of Axel F. Enström, the president of the academy. In 1924, Althin was hired as curator of
Tekniska Museet — which consisted of an empty desk in a corner of the library of the academy.
For the second time in only a few years, Althin began a nationwide search for artifacts of interest
from Sweden's technical and industrial history. His raids on Swedish factories soon gave him
the name "Sweden's biggest scrap merchant", but what he collected was not rubbish. At
Stjernsund Ironworks (which was founded by Christopher Polhem in 1699, and which was still
in operation at the time) Torsten Althin found, among other things, Polhem's gear-cutting
machine — an artifact that is unique in the history of technology.[30]

Contextual vs. Sequential: The Janus-Faced Heritage of Ethnology

Sigurd Erixon, the ethnologist at the Nordic Museum, became the role model for Althin when
he began to build his own museum in the late 1920s.[31] This meant that the ethnological principles
followed at the Nordic Museum in the 1920s, the philosophy of exhibiting artifacts, also became
the guidelines that shaped the interpretative philosophy of Tekniska Museet. The influence and
the time, i.e., the Nordic Museum and the 1920s, were crucial because had Tekniska Museet
been built in the 1890s it might well have been a completely different kind of museum.

The reason for this was that in the 1920s a long debate among Swedish ethnologists had
finally been settled. This debate had begun around 1900 when the building of the Nordic
Museum was completed, and concerned how the collected material was to be displayed. There
were two opposing traditions. The controversy is of some interest here, not only because the
outcome was to influence Tekniska Museet, and because it shows the ways in which museums
of technology are shaped by contemporary ideas, but because it concerns a major conceptual
choice which has to be made by any museum. Torsten Hägerstrand, the internationally
renowned Swedish human geographer,[32] has cited the clash of the two traditions as an example
of two fundamentally different ways of approaching reality conceptually: "The first is to
enclose a part of the world as it is found with its mixed assortment of beings, stationary and
mobile as the case may be. The second is to pick out in the mind classes of beings and 'remove'
them from their habitats and place them in a classification system."[33]

The first-mentioned tradition can be traced back to the philosophy of the creator of the
museum, Arthur Hazelius (1833-1901).[34] He had begun collecting artifacts of Swedish peasant
culture in the 1870s, when it was rapidly disappearing due to industrialisation. In 1873, he
opened a small museum of Scandinavian folklore in Stockholm. His basic idea was that artifacts

should be exhibited in their cultural contexts. The exhibition technique for this was the diorama: three-dimensional landscapes and interiors. He designed a set of tableaux of regional Swedish folk-life, complete with authentically costumed figures and appropriate artifacts. In 1876, Hazelius sent a set of six such tableaux to the Centennial Exhibition in Philadelphia: moose-hunting, courtship, christening, life among the Laplanders, Bible reading, and the death of a little girl. Work on the Nordic Museum began in 1888, but Hazelius' belief in the contextual approach, in exhibiting artifacts in their "natural habitat", led him also to collect entire buildings from throughout Sweden. In 1891 he opened Skansen, well-known today as "the prototype of all open-air museums".[35] (It was, for example, an idea that in the 1930s was successfully transplanted to Greenfield Village and Colonial Williamsburg in the United States.)

However, today's outstanding exponent in Sweden of the contextual perspective advocated by Hazelius during the last decades of the nineteenth century is probably the Biological Museum. It was opened in 1893, and although not originally an integrated part of Skansen it belongs to same period and tradition. The method employed by the Biological Museum was conceived by the taxidermist Gustaf Koltoff (1845-1913) as an alternative to the traditional practice of natural museums of the time, which was to place stuffed animals and birds together in show-cases and display cabinets according to classification principles. In the Biological Museum, Kolthoff attempted to display all the Scandinavian species, the whole fauna of animals and birds. The museum contained some two thousand species, all set in their natural habitat: a reconstructed landscape with a clever transition between the landscape in the foreground and the painted background (which was the work of the famous Swedish painter Bruno Liljefors, 1860-1939). The Biological Museum, located just outside Skansen, became the model for similar panoramas all over the world, including the American Museum of Natural History in New York.[36] Almost symbolically, its humble wooden facade faces the huge, imposing structure of the Nordic Museum on the other side of the road. However, the contextual tradition of the Biological Museum and Skansen was not able to cross the road and influence the Nordic Museum.

No, the Nordic Museum was to be dominated by another tradition. This tradition had its origin in an archaeological method that had emerged towards the end of the nineteenth century. The method was influenced by Darwin's theory of evolution and based upon the assumption that all artifacts had undergone an evolutionary process parallel to the evolution of organisms. In Sweden, it was introduced by the archaeologists Oscar Montelius (1843-1921) and Hans Hildebrand (1842-1913) who in the 1870s developed this into a rigid methodology, *"typology"*. By identifying the changing characteristics of a large number of artifacts, the artifacts could be arranged in "typological series", chains of development, which provided a relative chronology. Some early artifacts in a series could, for example, exhibit characteristics that were described as "rudimentary". In later objects in a series, features that had once filled a function became ornamental. The archaeologists tried to create longer and longer series by connecting separate chains through "missing links". Series of different kinds of artifacts, for example axes and buckles, could then be locked to one another on a relative time-scale if they were found together in the same strata at the same site. A few artifacts that could be dated with some certainty were then all that was needed to change this web of interconnected series, relative in time, into a firm grid that could be used for accurate dating.

All this was true (in principle at least) of the Stone Age and Bronze Age artifacts that Montelius, Hildebrand and their colleagues studied. But, as Hägerstrand writes, "at this time Darwin's theory of evolution had recently secured a footing in the Swedish academic world, far beyond the domains of biology".[37] Typology also became the scientific ideal of the ethnologists in their study of Scandinavian peasant culture. They rejected the idea of the diorama, and the reason was, according to Hägerstrand, that ethnology was at this time trying to become established as an academic discipline in the Swedish universities: "and to present objects arranged in dioramas did not correspond to the ethnologists' concept of truth and scholarly principles."[38] Their conceptual choice had major implications for the Nordic Museum, since, as Hägerstrand writes: "This view demanded that the objects of the museum ought to be arranged in terms of 'species groups', in other words, with all sickles and scythes in one place, all saddles together in another place and so on. The latter principle won the battle. The species classification came to dominate the museum until quite recently."[39]

Althin maintained strong links with Erixon and the other ethnologists at the Nordic Museum during the decades after 1936 when he began to furnish Tekniska Museet with permanent exhibitions.[40] This meant that Tekniska Museet did not choose the contextual approach, the dioramas of the Biological Museum and Hazelius' early version of the Nordic Museum. No, it was "all the sickles and scythes in one place, all the saddles together in another place" in Tekniska Museet, too. There were, for example, no dioramas of the Swedish ironworks — showing the crucial interdependence of technology, humans and the landscape in forests for charcoal, snow and ice for transportation, water for power and mines for metal — but artifacts and models of the iron and steel industry arranged in typological series in accordance with the principle of species classification, all proceeding from the "rudimentary" to the "ornamental".

It is easy to understand the conceptual choice of the Swedish ethnologists in their struggle for academic recognition during the early decades of the twentieth century. After all, as Hägerstrand writes, "the edifice of empirical science has been built almost exclusively on the base of classification of things and properties",[41] and they were probably prudent to subscribe to the dominant scientific ideal. However, the wisdom of their choice is worth pondering, since it also happened to influence the way Tekniska Museet interpreted technology, technological change and the social role of technology.

"The 'scientific' ethnologists failed to observe … that the diorama has a significance which is much deeper than just popular simplicity. The requirements to observe how a piece of a 'room' is totally filled up, forces one to reflect upon the consequences of … the local connections and the significance on the real world of continuity in space and time. When people and things are present together they have to do with each other and stand in proportion and power relations to each other in ways which cannot possibly be deduced from scientific laws and principles of the dominating kind."[42]

Not only Tekniska Museet, but most museums of technology apply the sequential perspective. They may scorn species classification as an outdated nineteenth-century exhibition technique, but they should all — even La Villette — be reminded that a basic structure of permanent exhibitions such as "Information Technology" is basically a species classification rather than a contextual approach.

The Shaping of History by the Present

In 1927, Oskar von Miller visited Stockholm. He had been invited by the Swedish-German friendship association to give a "Bericht über technische Museen".[43] On this occasion, von Miller was interviewed by a Swedish newspaper, and he expressed his satisfaction at being a member of the Royal Swedish Academy of Sciences: [44] "I'm a friend of Sweden in soul and heart", said von Miller. "It must have been an omen, that my father received the Vasa Order from the Swedish King Oscar on the day I was born".[45] During his visit to Stockholm, von Miller also visited the temporary exhibition of Tekniska Museet. Since the founding of the museum three years earlier, Torsten Althin had managed to arrange a small exhibition in the attic of the academy's house in central Stockholm which was open to the public on Sundays.

A few days later, a photo appeared in the press of von Miller posing in the modest exhibition with Althin and Enström.[46] Althin never missed an opportunity to hold up the Deutsches Museum as a model for a large Swedish technical museum, and von Miller's visit therefore served an important propaganda purpose. The model of the Deutsches Museum probably played a part in inducing a private foundation, Knut och Alice Wallenbergs Stiftelse, to donate two million Swedish crowns in 1933 for the erection a large museum building. Work on the museum, which had long been planned, could now commence. The museum was given the

Fig. 2 Oskar von Miller (left) on a visit in 1927 to the temporary exhibitions of the Tekniska Museet in the attic of the Royal Swedish Academy of Engineering Sciences, Stockholm. Torsten Althin, the director of the museum in the centre, and Axel F. Enström, the president of the academy, to the right. (Photo *Vecko-Journalen*, May 1, 1927)

barracks and grounds of a former household dragoon regiment, which had been made obsolete by the very technological development that the museum was intended to illustrate. On a day in July 1933, the regiment paraded for the last time and lowered its flag. On the next day, a group of serious-looking men in morning dress could be seen stalking over the empty barrack grounds.[47] In the centre of the group was Oskar von Miller, now seventy-eight years old, who happened to be visiting Stockholm again that summer, a year before his death. von Miller had come to participate in a biannual section meeting of the World Power Conference, and during his visit he was invited to inspect the site of the new museum in the company of his daughter and Conrad Matschoss (1871-1942), the German historian of technology.[48] Once again, the press had been notified and the photo appeared in many Swedish dailies.[49] On this occasion, von Miller was formally thanked by the president of the academy for his contribution to the development of the Swedish museum and he was made an honorary associate. After a long career in many fields, von Miller was replete with German and foreign honours. To be awarded this distinction by the as yet non-existant museum in the empty barracks (evacuated by the dragoons only the day before) may have meant little or nothing to him. This, however, like most marks of honour of this kind, was calculated to reflect more glory on the donors than the recipient. To the Swedish engineers, it served an important symbolic purpose to have the renowned Oskar von Miller – whose very name was synonymous with the Deutsches Museum — as the godfather of their own new museum.[50]

The site for the new museum building happened to be adjacent to the grounds where the Stockholm Exhibition had been held in 1930. This exhibition is well-known today in the history of architecture as one of the first and most distinct expressions of the international style which grew out of the *"Neue Sachlichkeit"* and which was shaped by architects such as Gropius, Le Corbusier and Mies. In Sweden the style became known at the Stockholm Exhibition of 1930 as *"Functionalism"* and the exhibition is considered one of the foremost works of its famous architect Gunnar Asplund (1885-1940).[51] The architect of Tekniska Museet, Ragnar Hjort (1887-1971), had also designed the museum in the functionalist style.[52] But even if the *form* of the museum was shaped by the functionalist movement, the *contents* — its division into various permanent exhibitions, the conceptual choices and interpretations — were shaped by other forces.[53]

The construction of the building began in the autumn of 1934, and early in 1936 work was accelerated, with the result that by the middle of May the building was more or less ready.[54] This was important, because it made it possible to hold the opening of the museum in conjunction with the seventy-fifth anniversary of the Swedish Society of Graduate Engineers on May 18, 1936. As mentioned above, a museum had been discussed when the society had planned its fiftieth anniversary twenty-five years earlier, but on that occasion they had settled for a *Festschrift* on Polhe. Now, however, the idea had materialised into a physical structure, although as yet devoid of contents. One of the few artifacts in the building during the opening ceremony was a huge steam engine, symbolically placed in the centre of the Grand Hall of Machinery, almost like an altar in a cathedral.[55] The museum was opened by Crown Prince Gustav Adolf (1882-1974, King Gustav VI Adolf 1950-1974) who pressed an electric button which set the huge steam engine in (artificial) motion. At this point, the entire Swedish Society of Graduate Engineers, the majority of the 1,400 people who filled the hall, rose from their seats and cheered.[56] The formal opening of the Deutsches Museum had occurred on the seventieth birthday of its founder, Oskar von Miller, whereas the opening of Tekniska Museet took place on the seventy-fifth birthday of the Swedish engineering society. This difference in symbolic timing illustrates that it was *their* museum more than anyone else's.

With the realisation of the dream of a large Swedish museum of technology, Swedish engineers at last had the means to overcome their alleged modesty, their reluctance to blow their own trumpet. The museum became, figuratively speaking, their own private international exhibition, an Olympic stadium of technology where they were their own judges and could award all the gold medals to Sweden. The largest gold medal of them all was, of course, conferred on Christopher Polhem. He had a permanent exhibition named after him, and one of his inventions became the logotype of the museum.

Fig. 3 From the opening ceremony in May 1936 of the new buildings of the Tekniska Museet. (Photo Tekniska Museet, Stockholm)

Torsten Althin told me many times that Oskar von Miller once said to him: "*Herr* Althin, whatever you do in Stockholm, never copy the Deutsches Museum".[57] What he had meant, Althin explained, was that the technical museums should have their own national style. But Althin told the story so many times, that I suspect he did so to counter any suspicion of the opposite being true. For a Swedish visitor to the Deutsches Museum today, at any rate, it is clear that Tekniska Museet was indeed modelled on the Deutsches Museum — although on a much smaller scale. It seems as if one has seen it all before, except that everything is so much larger and the objects so much more numerous in the Munich museum.[58] One feels, in fact, as one walks through the galleries, as if one is Gulliver in the land of the Giants.

You see, it was all here in the Swedish museum, at least in the Tekniska Museet that I grew up with in the 1950s, for example, a reconstruction of a mine in the cellar, a Grand Hall of Machinery devoted to prime movers and transportation, a Foucault's pendulum swinging through the main floors, and even a Swedish counterpart to the *Ehrensaal*, i.e., a marble gallery called *"Sverigesalen"* with busts and medallions of famous Swedish inventors and engineers.

Even if Tekniska Museet was more or less a copy of the Deutsches Museum, Althin did follow von Miller's advice to give the Swedish museum a distinct national character — but only in a literal respect. The Swedish museum lacked the ambition of the Deutsches Museum to present an international survey of technological development, and it became to a large extent a museum of Swedish industry. The division of the museum into permanent exhibitions mirrored the organisation of Swedish industry in interest groups for the various branches. This structure was a natural result of the fact that each branch organisation financed the furnishing of its own permanent exhibition in the decades that followed.[59] This was not a case of dubious, value-laden sponsorship as discussed in many museums today, but a simple economic reality since the Tekniska Museet was financed by Swedish industry. Had it not been for the support of industry, this symbol of the engineering profession would have remained an empty shell.

This had — at least from a historical point of view — a somewhat bizarre consequence. It was primarily those industrial sectors which were successful *at the time* that were able to have their history represented in the museum. Those branches of industry that showed less profit or that had run their natural course had their history neglected. The history of the past as represented by the museum became a reflection of the present, rather than an account of the development of Swedish industry and technology in a historical perspective. Tekniska Museet became a mirror image of contemporary Swedish industry.

There is, of course, no such thing as a "permanent exhibition". The museum has undergone a series of changes since the 1930s that reflect the changes of Swedish industry. For example, the textile industry exhibition, which was one of the larger permanent exhibitions in the 1950s, was closed down in the 1960s and a note placed on the door saying "Temporarily closed for renovation". At this time, the Swedish textile industry was being driven out of business by nations with lower labour costs, e.g., Portugal, India and the countries of South-east Asia. In a similar way, the exhibition on iron and steel was left intact for more than fifty years while the Swedish mining and metallurgy industry met fiercer and fiercer competition on the international market from nations such as Japan, and while the number of Swedish mines, blast furnaces and steelworks was being drastically reduced. Neither the textile industry nor the iron and steel industry had the means or the incentive to worry about their historical past. But at the same time, new or expanding industries were acquiring the means and the incentive to show their own history. For example, a new permanent exhibition on telecommunications was added in 1975, a section on computers in 1978, and a new exhibition on electrical power in 1983. Thus, the history of industries in decline constantly had to make way for the history of expanding ones.

History has been defined as "a dialogue between the present and the past about the future". But Tekniska Museet, to paraphrase this definition, became a monologue by the present about the future, disguised as the past; a monologue in perpetual change. In this, however, the Swedish museum is not unique. It is, I would like to argue, an intrinsic problem in any museum of technology. As one passes through the halls and galleries of any museum of technology — be it in Sweden or abroad — and smells the wet paint and sees a new, *à la mode* permanent exhibition, one may rest assured that this is an exhibition tracing the origins and historical development of an industry which is flourishing today. Conversely, outmoded historical exhibitions — where the dust is thick, where the sign "Temporarily out of order" has taken on a permanent look, and where the little plastic letters on the labels have been allowed to fall to the floor and be lost — always portray industries that are themselves in a state of decline. In fact, museums of technology may be an unsuspected source of information for investors on the stock exchange!

But this phenomenon is too important to be dismissed in jest. The reasons are not simply financial, but concern a more profound difference in how we view technological change. Many historians tend to regard museums of technology as exploiters rather than as explainers of history, and in this monologue by the present about the future, history, they argue, seems to be distorted.[60] This, however, does not worry museum curators in general because that is just what most museums of technology see as their function: to explain the present and to prepare us for the future.[61] Not only is this true today, it has been the ambition of most museums of technology throughout the twentieth century.[62] To them, the use of history is only one of many educational means of achieving their ambition. The paradox is only there for those of us who are trained or inclined to believe that a museum should in some sense give a balanced account of the entire historical process (for the period, nation/area and topic covered by the name or the statutes of the museum). That is, that each branch or field of technology should have a permanent exhibition occupying a proportion of the whole museum that corresponds to its relative importance in the general, total historical development. But this is by no means self-evident.

It only seems so to those of us who tend to view museums as three-dimensional general survey textbooks, who approach museums of technology from the perspective of history rather than from the perspective of modern industry and contemporary issues.

This problem, I would like to suggest, presents any museum of technology with a major conceptual choice. To define this dichotomy I will introduce two rather awkward concepts: archaeocentric and contempocentric. Should the perspective be *archaeocentric,* i.e., should the museum try to give a balanced account of the historical development of various technologies and their relative importance in the past — regardless of their strength and importance today? Or should a museum of technology employ a *contempocentric* perspective, i.e., should the museum attempt primarily to trace the origins and the historical development of the technologies that are important today — and that may be even more so tomorrow? It would be an oversimplification to use the terms "historic" and "contemporary" to explain this difference,[63] because the perspective is historical in both cases. The difference lies in the vantage point, the mental outlook. The museums of technology of the twentieth century have by and large employed a contempocentric perspective, and this will always confuse some visitors (historians in particular) who expect to find an archaeocentric perspective and a traditional historical museum. Since the vantage point constantly changes in a contempocentric perspective, museums of technology will constantly be questioned, challenged and redesigned.

Fig. 4 The main building of the Tekniska Museet, Stockholm, built in 1936. (Photo Stockholm Stadsmuseum, Stockholm)

Conclusions

Museums are, as we know, artifacts in their own right, cultural objects shaped by the contemporary social context. Each museum of technology is the product of a historical process, a process which influences and shapes the conceptual choices made in its design. There are, this paper suggests, three conceptual choices to be made by any museum of technology, and the characteristics of each museum can be described in terms of these dichotomies:

International	-	National
Contextual	-	Sequential
Archaeocentric	-	Contempocentric

The paper has described the historical process that led Sweden's Tekniska Museet to make conceptual choices that placed the museum more or less in the right-hand column of this matrix: its perspectives became basically national, sequential and contempocentric. Any museum of technology, I would like to suggest, can be defined in terms of this matrix. A museum of technology does not, *nota bene*, necessarily have to plump for one or the other alternative in any particular perspective, it may very well try to achieve a balanced mix between the two. However, should there be inherent tensions within a museum of technology with regard to its exhibition policy, these tensions may perhaps be attributed to the fact that one of the conceptual choices in the figure is either unresolved or not elucidated.

The strength of the Deutsches Museum was, perhaps, that it was a successful blend of all these perspectives. It provided an international as well as a national perspective, it had contextual dioramas as well as sequential displays, and it gave historical surveys as well as highlighting the origins of modern technologies. Its contemporaries and imitators may all have failed to establish this balance by opting for extreme conceptual choices or by failing to clarify them in their own minds. Is this the reason why the colossus on the *Museumsinsel* in the Isar still captivates all of us, regardless of our own perspective?

Notes

1   Parts of this article were first included in a talk in German, given at the Deutsches Museum in Munich on September 11, 1985. A version of the talk was subsequently published in Swedish, see: Svante Lindqvist, "Deutsches Museum, Tekniska Museet och bilden av Polhem", *Daedalus* (Yearbook of Tekniska Museet) 54 (1985), pp. 165-173. Earlier versions of this paper were presented in seminars at the Eleutherian-Hagley Museum, Delaware, on March 25, 1987, and at the National Museum of American History in Washington, D.C., on July 28, 1987. For valuable comments on earlier versions, I am indebted in particular to Eugene S. Ferguson and David A. Hounshell. I would also like to acknowledge the help I have received from Margareta Bond-Fahlberg, librarian at the Royal Institute of Technology.

2   Torsten Althin, "An Intellectual Autobiography", *Technology and Culture* 20 (1979), p. 589.

3   Primarily with American scholars in the Society for the History of Technology (S.H.O.T.), such as Eugene S. Ferguson, Melvin Kranzberg, Robert P. Multhauf and Cyril Stanley Smith, but also with D.S.L. Cardwell, Richard L. Hills and other British historians of technology in the Newcomen Society. See: Royal Institute of Technology Library, Stockholm, Althin Papers, Correspondence 1964-1981.

4   For a description of the main European museums of technology in 1925, see: Charles R. Richards, *The Industrial Museum*. New York, Macmillan, 1925. For a general historical background to technical museums, see: Friedrich Klemm, "Geschichte der naturwissenschaftlichen und technischen Museen", *Deutsches Museum, Abhandlungen und Berichte* 41 (1973), Heft 2.

5   For a history of the background and early years of the museum, see: Conrad Matschoss, *Das*

Deutsche Museum: Geschichte, Aufgaben, Ziele. Berlin & München, VDI-Verlag & R. Oldenbourg, 1925. See also J. Zenneck, *Fünfzig Jahre Deutsches Museum München,* München. Deutsches Museum, 1953.

6   *Nya Dagligt Allehanda,* June 6, 1926. Original in Swedish: *"Sverige illa representerat på Deutsches Museum. Ingenjörsvetenskapsakademien har sin uppmärksamhet fäst å saken".*

7   *Industritidningen Norden* 1926, September. Original in Swedish: *"Knapphändigt representerat, delvis utan nationalitetsetikett".*

8   *Nya Dagligt Allehanda,* June 6, 1926. Original in Swedish: *"vi svenskar äro för blygsamma, för obenägna att en smula slå på trumman för oss själva och vårt eget".*

9   Conrad Matschoss, *Männer der Technik.* München, Verein Deutscher Ingenieure, 1925.

10   Eugene S. Ferguson, "Technical Museums and International Exhibitions", *Technology and Culture* 6 (1965), pp. 30-46.

11   Richard Espy, *The Politics of the Olympic Games.* Berkeley, University of California Press, 1979, p. 164. Cf. Allen Guttmann, *The Games Must Go On: Avery Brundage and the Olympic Movement.* New York, Columbia University Press, 1984. — A Swedish connection between industry and the Olympic Games is provided by J. Sigfrid Edström (1870-1964). Trained as an electrical engineer, he was vice president of the electrical power company ASEA, one of Sweden's largest export companies, from 1903-1933. He was also a member of the Executive Board of the International Olympic Committee from 1921-1952 and its vice president from 1937-1942. From 1946-1952, he was Avery Brundage's predecessor as chairman of the I.O.C. Cf. Guttmann, *passim.*

12   Cf. Folke T. Kihlstedt, "Utopia Realized: The World's Fairs of the 1930s", in: Joseph J. Corn, ed., *Imagining Tomorrow: History, Technology, and the American Future.* Cambridge, Mass., The MIT Press, 1986, pp. 97-136.

13   R. Espy, *op. cit.,* 1979, p. 164.

14   *The Fifth Olympiad: The Official Report of the Olympic Games of Stockholm 1912,* issued by the Swedish Olympic Committee, edited by Erik Bergvall, translated by Edward Adams-Ray. Stockholm, Wahlström & Widstrand, 1913.

15   A modern comparison would be the heavy volumes of the *Science Citation Index* that can be found today in all research libraries around the world, but here the number of citations is seen as a sign of individual merit rather than as a contribution to national prestige.

16   See, for example, *Göteborgs Handels- och Sjöfarts-Tidning,* May 8, 1925.

17   Tekniska Museets arkiv, Stockholm: Torsten Althin, "Resan till invigningen av Deutsches Museums nya byggnader i München, maj 1925" (typewritten MS, 1 p.).

18   Torsten Althin, "Ett tekniskt museum: Svenska Teknologföreningens jubileumstanke år 1911", *Daedalus* (Yearbook of Tekniska Museet) 44 (1974), pp. 11-22; Richard Smedberg, "Tekniska museet", *ibid.,* pp. 23-35.

19   Bo Sundin, *Ingenjörsvetenskapens tidevarv: Ingenjörsvetenskapsakademien, Pappersmassekontoret, Metallografiska institutet och den tekniska forskningen i början av 1900-talet* (Acta Universitatis Umensis, Umeå Studies in the Humanities, No. 42, Umeå, 1981). English summary on pp. 207-218.

20   Although the museum was founded in 1924, the museum building was not opened until 1936.

21   *Christopher Polhem: Minnesskrift utgifven av Svenska Teknologföreningen* (Stockholm, 1911). It was translated into English and published in the United States some fifty years after its original publication, see: *Christoper Polhem: The Father of Swedish Technology,* transl. by William A. Johnsson. Hartford, Conn., 1963.

22   For an autobiographical article in English, see Althin 1979, pp. 583-589. For biographical articles in Swedish, see: Hans Hylander, "Om och till Torsten Althin" in: Nicolai Herlofson et al., eds, *Vilja och kunnande: Teknikhistoriska uppsatser tillägnade Torsten Althin på hans åttioårsdag den 11 juli 1977 av vänner.* Uppsala, 1977, pp. 9-18; Svante Lindqvist, "Torsten Althin in memoriam", *Daedalus* (Yearbook of Tekniska Museet) 51 (1982), pp. 9-12.

23   This, and the following anecdotes in this paragraph, are based on personal communication from Torsten Althin.

24   Torsten Althin, *op. cit.,* 1979, p. 586.

25   Cf. Thomas P. Hughes, *American Genesis: A Century of Invention and Technological Enthusiasm 1870-1970.* New York, Viking Penguin, 1989.

26   Hans Hylander, *op. cit.,* 1977, pp. 10-11.

27   Personal communication from Torsten Althin.

28   Personal communication from Torsten Althin. Original in Swedish: *"ett hejdundrande fiasko".*

29   For a description of the collection, see: Edvard Hubendick, "Industrihistoriska samlingarna på jubileumsutställningen i Göteborg", *Teknisk Tidskrift, Allmänna avdelningen* 1923, No. 31 (August 4), pp. 238-242. Today, this collection forms the nucleus of the present Museum of Industrial History in Gothenburg.

30 Dr. Michael Lindgren, curator at Tekniska Museet, is working on a forthcoming study on Polhem and his manufacturing technology.
31 A somewhat macabre demonstration of this can be found in the columbarium of the Engelbrekt church in Stockholm where Sigurd Erixon was buried in 1968. Althin once told me (this must have been in the late 1970s) that he had bought the box next to Erixon so that they would rest side by side. And so they have rested since 1982, the teacher and his pupil from the Nordic Museum in 1920.
32 Internationally, Hägerstrand is perhaps best known for his pioneering study in 1953 on the diffusion of innovations as a spatial process (an English translation was published by the University of Chicago Press in 1967). Cf. Allan Pred, ed., *Space and Time in Geography: Essays Dedicated to Torsten Hägerstrand*, Lund Studies in Geography, Ser. B, Human Geography No. 48. Lund, Gleerup, 1981.
33 Torsten Hägerstrand, "Presence and Absence: A Look at Conceptual Choices and Bodily Necessities", *Regional Studies*, Vol. 18.5 (1983), pp. 373-380, quote on p. 374. I am indebted to Karen Wonders for drawing my attention to this article.
34 For literature on Hazelius and his work in English, see: Nils-Arvid Bringeus, "Arthur Hazelius and the Nordic Museum", *Ethnologica Scandinavia* 3 (1974), pp. 5-16; Bo Lagercrantz, "A Great Museum Pioneer of the Nineteenth Century", *Curator* 7 (1964), No. 3, pp. 179-184; Mats Rehnberg, *The Nordiska Museet and Skansen*. Stockholm, Nordiska Museet, 1957. Cf. Arne Biörnstad, ed., *Skansen under hundra år*. Höganäs, Wiken, 1991.
35 Jay Anderson, *Time Machines: The World of Living History*. Nashville, American Association for State and Local History, 1984, p. 17. Cf. *idem, The Living History Sourcebook*, Nashville, American Association for State and Local History, 1985, pp. 3-4.
36 This, at least, is the prevailing opinion in Sweden. Karen Wonders, a doctoral candidate at the Department of Art History at the University of Uppsala, is presently working on a history of dioramas that will put the Biological Museum and its role in the larger perspective of contemporary European and North American museums. She has published two articles on aspects of the dioramas, see: Karen Wonders, "Exhibiting Fauna — From Spectacle to Habitat Group", *Curator* 32 (1989), No. 2, pp. 131-156; Karen Wonders, "The Illusionary Art of Background Painting in Habitat Dioramas", *Curator* 33 (1990), No. 2, pp. 90-117.
37 Torsten Hägerstrand, *op. cit.*, 1983 p. 375.
38 *Loc. cit.*
39 *Ibid.*, pp. 375-376. — In the 1970s, however, the contextual approach found its way into the Nordic Museum in exhibitions such as *"Resa i Sverige"* (Travelling in Sweden) in 1974.
40 Althin told me that he once a week used to walk from Tekniska Museet to a restaurant at Skansen to participate in the weekly lunch of Erixon and his group. The importance of these lunches as well as Althin's regular attendance is confirmed in Biörnstad 1991, p. 105.
41 Torsten Hägerstrand, *op. cit.*, 1983, p. 374.
42 *Ibid.*, p. 376.
43 *Svenska Dagbladet*, April 23, 1927.
44 The Royal Swedish Academy of Sciences, founded in 1739, should not be confused with the Royal Swedish Academy of Engineering Sciences, founded in 1919. The former is internationally better known, having awarded the Nobel prizes in physics and chemistry since 1901. Von Miller was a foreign member of both academies.
45 *Op. cit.* Original in Swedish: *"Jag är Sverigevän av själ och hjärta. Ett omen var det väl, att samma dag jag föddes fick min far Vasaorden av kung Oscar"*
46 *Vecko-Journalen*, May 1, 1927.
47 *Stockholms Tidningen-Stockholms Dagblad*, July 3, 1933.
48 Conrad Matschoss is primarily known today for his *Die Entwicklung der Dampfmaschine*, 2 Vols. Berlin, Springer 1908. For an assessment of his work, see: Ulrich Troitzsch & Gabriele Wohlauf, eds., *Technik-Geschichte: Historische Beiträge und neuere Ansätze*. Frankfurt am Main, Suhrkamp, 1980, pp. 81-91.
49 See, for example, *Skaraborgs Tidningen*, July 5, 1933.
50 Sigurd Erixon said this indirectly in an article on *Tekniska Museet* which was published in a *Festschrift* on the occasion of the seventyfifth anniversary of the engineering society in 1936, see: *Teknisk Tidskrift: Festskrift till Svenska Teknologföreningens 75-årsjubileum 1861-1935*. Stockholm, Svenska Teknologföreningen, 1936, p. 16.
51 Per G. Råberg, *Funktionalistiskt genombrott: Radikal miljö och miljödebatt i Sverige 1925-1931*, Stockholm, Norstedt, 1972. Cf. T.P. Hughes, *op. cit.*, 1989, pp. 309-324.
52 Tomas Mjöberg, "Tekniska Museets byggnad och dess tillkomsthistoria", *Daedalus* (Yearbook of Tekniska Museet) 54 (1985), pp. 175-187.
53 In 1936, Sigurd Erixon stated the philosophy that was to govern the furnishing of Tekniska Museet, see: Sigurd Erixon, *op. cit.*, 1936, pp. 19-20.

54 Torsten Althin, "Tekniska Museets byggnad: IV. Byggnadsarbetet under 1936", *Daedalus* (Yearbook of Tekniska Museet) 7 (1937), p. 34.
55 Christian Laine has pointed out that the monumental design of Tekniska Museet was in the tradition of the large art galleries, going back to Museo Pio-Clementino in the Vatican from the end of the eighteenth century: a centrepiece, which is the symbolic and visual climax of the collection, positioned on the main axis through the museum and the entrance. See: Christian Laine, "De nya museerna", *Daedalus* (Yearbook of Tekniska Museet) 54 (1985), p. 146.
56 Personal communication from Torsten Althin.
57 Quoted after Torsten Althin, *op. cit.*, 1979, p. 588.
58 The total area of Tekniska Museet in 1936 was 9,000 m^2, of which 5,200 m^2 was exhibition area. The exhibition area of the Deutsches Museum in 1925 was 36,000 m^2 – i.e., seven times larger.
59 This process took some time, and the entire area of the museum was not filled with permanent exhibitions until the 1950s. In the 1960s older exhibitions began to be closed down, and in the 1970s they made way for new permanent exhibitions. Three more buildings were added in the 1970s and early 1980s: the two remaining stables of the former dragoon regiment became wings of the main museum building, containing the new permanent exhibitions on telecommunications, computers and electrical power. A third building, the riding school of the regiment, became a science centre.
60 For a well-articulated example of this opinion among historians, see: George Basalla, "Museums and Technological Utopianism", *Curator* 17 (1974), pp. 106-107.
61 Victor J. Danilov, the foremost spokesman of the science centre movement, formulated the role of this new kind of museum in the following way: "They are concerned with furthering public understanding and appreciation of the physical and life sciences, engineering, technology, industry and, health and seek to accomplish this goal by making museums both enlightening and entertaining. They are best known for their *contemporary* rather than *historic* perspective and their reliance on participatory exhibit techniques rather than objects of intrinsic value" (emphasis added), in: Victor J. Danilov, *Science and Technology Centers*. Cambridge, Mass., The MIT Press, 1982, Preface.
62 Charles R. Richards, for example, in his influential book *The Industrial Museum*, written in 1925, defined the aims of the museums of technology as follows: "The processes of production that underlie the civilisation of today are hidden behind factory walls where only the specialised factory worker enters. Little is known about these operations by the growing boy and girl. To attempt to present these things through books is unsatisfactory and tame. The processes must be revealed to the eye and set forth in the simplest and clearest possible fashion if the foundations of our present-day life are not only to be understood, but to become an element in the culture of today. The industrial museum in its highest development endeavours to accomplish this purpose by displays of materials that clearly and succinctly illustrate industrial processes in ways that may be readily understood by both young and old. If it be granted that this educational aim is the paramount purpose of an industrial museum and its theme the industrial basis of our present-day life, it is important to... ", in: Charles R. Richards, *op. cit.*, pp. 1-2.
63 Cf. emphasis in n. 61.

CLEAN EXHIBITS, MESSY EXHIBITS: HENRY FORD'S TECHNOLOGICAL AESTHETIC

John M. Staudenmaier, S.j.

University of Detroit Mercy, U.S.A.

Unlike the other major technological museums of the Western world, the Henry Ford Museum and Greenfield Village and its massive collections manifest the driving purpose of a single person. During the relatively brief period spent shopping in England and the United States in the late 1920s for relics of the industrial revolution, Henry Ford dominated the design process down to minute levels of detail. The team of Ford Motor Company employees assigned to constructing the village learned early that it did not pay to settle an antique building on too permanent a foundation. Mr. Ford might change his mind tomorrow and order it moved to a new spot on the site. The entire project, from the architecture of the museum and layout of the village to the contents of the collection and the aesthetic style of their presentation, forms a coherent representation of one very powerful man's vision of the technological shaping of the modern world.[1]

All this makes the Ford complex very helpful if one seeks complicated, but manageable, cases for studying powerful technologies as cultural symbols. Since museums are in the business of interpreting and constructing symbols, the Ford story fits the purposes of The Cité's conference aptly. When looked at in terms of symbolic meaning, the relationship between Henry Ford, the person, and his two major achievements in the twenties, the Rouge and the museum-village, is full of surprises. For this essay I have arranged some of them into a set of four hypotheses which help make sense of Ford's ambiguous symbolic character. I am less concerned, however, with the particularities of the Ford story than with a critical challenge facing technical museums which those particularities illustrate.

"Should museums create clean or messy technological exhibits?" The four hypotheses which follow are themselves "messy" in the sense that they would be very difficult to prove. Still, one can argue in their defence that they give shape to a set of circumstances, decisions and events typical of the elusive processes by which very successful technologies, and technologists, acquire symbolic meaning.

HYPOTHESIS 1:

In 1930 the Rouge Plant, not the Ford Museum -
Greenfield Village complex, was the real museum.

In October 1929 Henry Ford opened the only partially complete Edison Institute with a ceremony of extravagant homage to his revered octogenarian friend, Thomas Edison. "Light's Golden Anniversary" marked the Edison team's successful testing of an incandescent light bulb fifty years before to the day. Ford invited hundreds of the wealthiest scions of the industrial era to a banquet in the massive foyer of the partially completed museum building. The gala began next door in Greenfield Village's reconstructed Menlo Park complex. Ford and President Hoover looked on as Edison turned on a replica of the first lamp while the nation listened over a live NBC radio hookup.[2]

Despite the massive publicity of its inaugural event, the museum and village did not open to the public for four more years. Ford founded a small trade school for boarders, but visitors were apparently admitted on a random basis until early 1933 when Ford was finally convinced by thousands of requests to build a gatehouse and begin a paid admission policy for the general public.[3] From the thirties until 1980, moreover, the museum and village maintained a reputation as dominated by antiquarian Ford afficionados.[4]

Only a few miles away, meanwhile, the sprawling River Rouge plant belched plumes of smoke and streams of motorised vehicles from the largest manufacturing operation on earth. The Rouge contrasted with the museum-village complex on almost every level and the contrasts are instructive. While the museum-village remained a private enclave, the Rouge offered guided tours to the public. Some 500,000 people thronged to see the apotheosis of modern technology annually. The plant served, one could argue, as the largest and most popular working exhibit ever dreamt of in the history of technical museums.

The Rouge's symbolic power stirred hearts far beyond the borders of Detroit. The factory became something of a pilgrims' shrine for Europeans, in particular from the Weimar Republic. Deeply emotional, quasi-religious responses were not unusual. German engineer Otto Moog recorded his impressions in a language that combines intimidation with an exultant sense of liberation in almost schizoid fashion. "No symphony, no *Eroica*, compares in depth, content, and power to the music *that threatened and hammered away at us* as we wandered through Ford's workplaces, *wanderers overwhelmed* by a *daring expression of the human spirit.*"[5]

Mexican muralist Diego Rivera echoes the same sentiments. Ruminating on the power of the Rouge which he was soon to immortalise in his Detroit Institute of Art murals, he speaks of the achievement of production workers in the same breath as he refers to an almost preternatural power that transcends individual human agency altogether. "I thought of the millions of different men by whose combined labor and thought automobiles were produced, from the miners who dug the iron ore out of the earth to the railroad men and teamsters who brought the finished machines to the consumer, so that man, space, and time might be conquered, *and ever-expanding victories be won against death...*"[6]

Rivera's rhetoric ("so that *man*, space and time might be conquered") salts his optimistic rationalism of technology conquering nature with the ominous hint that humans serve more as victims than as masters of progress. Rivera was a Marxist; his affective response to the Rouge, as a triumphant industrial achievement, was accordingly less surprising than his equally powerful feelings for Henry Ford himself. In his autobiography, he compares the factory to an orchestra with Ford as the daring new composer. "As I rode back to Detroit (from lunch with H. Ford), a vision of Henry Ford's industrial empire kept passing before my eyes. In my ears, I heard the wonderful symphony which came from his factories where metals were shaped into tools for man's service. *It was a new music, waiting for the composer with genius enough to give it communicable form...* I regretted that Henry Ford was a capitalist and one of the richest men on earth. I did not feel free to praise him as long and as loudly as I wanted to, since that would put me under the suspicion of sycophancy, of flattering the rich. Otherwise, I should have attempted to write a book presenting *Henry Ford as I saw him, a true poet and artist, one of the greatest in the world.*"[7] (emphasis mine)

For Rivera, Ford incarnated the dream that rationality, embodied in machine technology, would liberate humanity from the sufferings of burdensome nature and the debilities of constricting tradition.

Fig. 1 Aerial view of the River Rouge Plant. (Courtesy of the collections of Henry Ford Museum & Greenfield Village)

There are at work here three identifiable symbols which overlap so much that, even though they are distinct, it is difficult to identify their conceptual boundaries. Where, one asks when reading such emotion-laden responses as these, does the mythic "Henry Ford" blur into the preternatural force of "Fordism"? How much do both of these presences within early twentieth century Western culture depend on the massive physical presence of "The Rouge" as the shrine and sacrament of the modern age? The Rouge attracted its half million pilgrims each year for the same reason, ultimately, that people visit technical museums generally. They come to be in the presence of the artifacts that have shaped their history and their world, to feel and smell and see and listen to them.

But if the Rouge, according to the interpretation I am arguing, is the real museum, how ought we understand Ford's extraordinary investment of money and personal energy in what we now call the museum and the village?

HYPOTHESIS 2:

The museum and village provided Henry with a safe haven from the Rouge.

A great deal of evidence suggests that Henry Ford himself shared the intimidation expressed by so many other visitors to the Rouge and that he constructed the museum and village as a private refuge. In part Ford held aloof from Detroit's wealthy elites for whom he remained an awkward outsider. Fairlane, the Ford mansion completed in 1916, stood on the banks of the Rouge river in working class Dearborn, miles from the high society of Grosse Pointe's mansion row. In part he retreated from his own monstrous corporation.

When Henry Ford began to purchase approximately 2,000 acres along the banks of the Rouge river in 1915, he already possessed a household name. More than half the autos sold in the United States were Model T's. The "T" matched the existing U.S. market better, perhaps, than any technology ever has; it combined durable construction and a high centre of gravity with simplicity and ease of repair, all attractive qualities in an era when the majority of roads went unpaved and a network of maintenance facilities was non-existent. Farmers, in particular, proved a nearly insatiable market. Ford's simultaneous inauguration of the moving assembly line and the $5.00 day the year before had infuriated his competitors while it astonished and edified the public and won him the reputation of industrial genius and working-man's friend. Ford cut the work day from nine to eight hours while approximately doubling the daily wage to $5.00.

Less publically visible was his obsession with control. Thus, the labour reform package raised wages to $5.00 per day by adding a "profit sharing" bonus but it required that workers qualify for it by passing a home visit inspection. Members of the newly created Sociological Department checked for cleanliness, debt, drinking habits and a list of other equally intimate matters. A failing grade meant that the profit sharing bonus was put in escrow until the worker mended his ways. Failure to comply eventually meant firing.[8] The design of the Rouge itself — its access to Great Lakes shipping lanes and intersecting rail lines, its dramatically expanded capacities for primary input manufacture — sought to vertically integrate a wholly-owned, mine-mouth-to-dealership production unit.[9]

Ford's dream of total control showed itself in other key areas during the years that the Rouge was being completed. After his humiliation during the 1919 *Chicago Tribune* trial, his reclusive tendencies deepened.[10] Thus, in the same year, after major stockholders had sued (and won) because of Ford's practice of ploughing profits back into company expansion, Ford designed an elaborate and deceptive strategy for buying them out; he completed the transactions in July of 1919. Almost simultaneously, three of "his ablest lieutenants" (C. Harold Wills, John R. Lee,

Fig. 2 Exterior shot of the Henry Ford Museum under construction. (Courtesy of the collections of Henry Ford Museum & Greenfield Village)

Norval Hawkins) resigned under pressure.[11] Thomas Hughes has suggested that Ford's increasingly autocratic managerial style reflects his inability to make the transition from the intimate scale of operations at the 1906 Piquette Street plant to the colossus on the Rouge river. The workforce at Piquette Street had been so small, and highly innovative operations so informal, that Ford could relate with everyone in folksy comfort.[12] The team of Ford Motor Company workers who were assigned to work on the museum and village project look a great deal more like Piquette Street than they do the Rouge. Tales abound of familiar, though hardly peer, interactions between Ford and his boys.

The museum and village romanticise industrialisation by lionising heroic individuals in the village and by detaching artifacts from their contexts. There is, for example, no hint of the moving assembly line whose financial success made the entire complex fiscally possible. Edward Cutler, who oversaw the construction of the village, recalled years later his intuition that Mr. Ford sought out the village as a retreat from the corporation.

"I believe the pressures of Mr. Ford's work were relieved by the work in Greenfield Village and my office. The office and his work in the Village were safety valves for the pressure and strain of the Ford Motor Company. He spent so much time around the village. Several times he would make a crack: 'Well, I guess I'll have to leave you now, and go and make some more money for us to spend down here.'

It was a relief for him to get down here. For years he wouldn't let me have a telephone. When I would ask him about it, and I had a lot of running around to do, he would say, 'Oh, forget that stuff. I come down here to get away from that gang.' He didn't want any way for them to get a hold of him."[13]

HYPOTHESIS 3:

Ford's aesthetic, "the clean machine", flees the Rouge by sanitizing the technological process.

Given Ford's penchant for control and his solipsistic tendencies, it is not surprising that his aesthetic for technological display should take a form of sanitized machinery portrayed in abstraction from its working context. The museum and village embody this motif by combining a powerful strain of romantic nostalgia with an equally powerful commitment to contemporary technocratic motifs. Greenfield Village ignored twentieth century technologies almost completely and, indeed, made expensive hash of any historical chronology. Ford bought what he liked and installed it. Shrines to American heroes dotted the landscape: Abraham Lincoln's early court house, homes of Noah Webster, Ford himself, the Wright brothers, and the jewel of the collection, a worshipful reincarnation of the laboratory complex at Menlo Park where Thomas Edison had invented the electric light a half century before.

The adjacent museum aimed more at aesthetically pleasing arrays of artifacts (most notably: steam engines, automobiles, locomotives, agricultural equipment, machine tools, and domestic appliances), each series arranged in chronologically ascending order to demonstrate the march of inventive progress. Thus the historically specific working context of each machine was replaced by a progressivist context in which design changes follow one another with seeming inevitability, where no design change appears to result from the political, cultural or ideological forces at work in the artifact's context of origin.

In almost every other part of his domain, Ford displayed large machines as sensuous, almost numinous, icons. In the village, he ordered the walls opening into the steam engine rooms of the Loringer gristmill and adjacent Armington and Sims machine shop changed from the original wood to glass so that he could watch the machines function as he passed by. The powerhouse at the Highland Park plant (*c.* 1910) was exhibited to Woodward Avenue passers-

Fig. 3 Interor shot of the Henry Ford Museum under construction. (Courtesy of the collections of Henry Ford Museum & Greenfield Village)

by through walls of showroom glass; inside, the dynamos were enthroned amid gleaming brass and tile. Not a few observers have noted that Ford's secluded "Fairlane" estate (*c.* 1916) could boast of only one really elegant building, the hydro-power plant, a shrine to dynamos very like Highland Park's.[14]

One of the Rouge's design departures from its predecessor at Highland Park would later become a world famous symbol of Ford's rejection of debate and dissent. Just as Ford pursued integrated control of inputs through his network of transportation lines converging on the Rouge, so he sought even more control over workers than the house-to-house inspections and in-factory spy networks of the 1914 labour reforms had offered. Highland Park opened directly on Woodward Avenue, leaving Ford management with no say about who mingled with workers on the public streets fronting the factory. Plant accessibility meant unwanted interference. In dramatic contrast, the new Rouge compound was insulated by a fully fenced perimeter and tightly guarded gates. The Miller Road Gate No. 4 became world infamous when photographers caught Ford thugs beating United Auto Worker activists Walter Reuther and Richard Frankenstein in 1937's "battle of the overpass". Independent minded workers seeking to organise a union were anathema to Ford, they apotheosised the intrusion of pluralism into the ideologically standardised interior of the Ford universe.

Ford's aesthetic, in short, showed itself not only in design choices affecting the display of sensuous and elegant machines but also in the seemingly pragmatic design decisions that determined architecture as well. In this regard, the layout of the new Ford Museum would consistently echo the Rouge's dedication to control over workers. Architect Robert O. Derrick was hired to design the museum building. In his oral history interviews he recounts his conversation with Ford about the museum's floor plan. "He said we would have to have a model (of the proposed Ford Museum building) made, so we had a model made and it showed the balconies, naturally, and the basement, and he said, 'What is this up here?' I said, 'That is a balcony for exhibit'. He said, '*I wouldn't have that; there would be people up there, I could come in and they wouldn't be working. I wouldn't have it.*' He said, '*I have to see everybody.*' Then he said, 'What's this?' I said, 'That is the basement down there, which is necessary to maintain these exhibits and to keep things which you want to rotate, etc.' He said, '*I wouldn't have that; I coudn't see those men down there when I came in.* You have to do the whole thing over again and put it on one floor with no balconies and no basement.' I said , 'Okay.'"[15]

Ford's industrial aesthetic, so like the design of the Rouge plant in its avoidance of the messy political side of technology can be understood as the eccentric aberrations of a man whose rise to fame and fortune permitted him to indulge in a growing obsession with privacy and personal control. From another perspective, however, Ford's ambivalent mix of liberation and repression, so aptly captured by Otto Moog and similarly articulate visitors to the Rouge, fits quite closely other idealisations of progress in the twenties and thirties. Perhaps the most striking symbolic representation of popular ambivalence about technological triumphs would appear in the main foyer of the Hall of Science at the 1933-34 Chicago "Century of Progress" Exposition. The Exposition's upbeat tone and theme stood in stark contradiction against the background of its historical context; 1934 marked the savage depths of the nation's worst depression. Visitors to the Fair's Hall of Science were met in the foyer by the "Fountain of Science" with Louise Lentz Woodruff's three-piece sculpture, "Science Advancing Mankind". Two life-sized figures, male and female, faced forward with arms uplifted. Both were dwarfed by the massive figure of a metallic robot twice their size. In the words of Lenox Lohr, general manager of the exposition, the robot typified "the exactitude, force and onward movement of science, with its hands at the backs of the figures of a man and a woman, urging them on to the fuller life". The sculpture's iconographic ideology was reinforced by the official Guidebook's stunning, bold-faced thematic motto: "SCIENCE FINDS, INDUSTRY APPLIES, MAN CONFORMS."[16]

The Chicago Fair's technocratic ideal is rooted in a violent disjunction between the combined force of "Science" and "Industry" (itself a conflation of business and technology) on the one side and "Man" on the other. The role of "Man" in the modernist equation is not to "*Critique*" fallible decisions made by scientists, business managers or engineers; it is not even to "*Use*" the new technologies. The role of "Man" is to "*Conform*".[17]

HYPOTHESIS 4:

The penchant in technological museums for clean, rather than messy exhibits, marks museum designers as Fordist.

These are explosive issues; Ford's sanitised aesthetic, after all, comes uncomfortably close to much contemporary technical museum practice. Does the typical iconography of technological exhibitions, replete with splendid mechanisations but devoid of disturbing symbols of oppression, reflect a cultural inhibition about facing the trade-offs inherent in technological choices? In 1989 David Harvey called attention to the role museums can and often do play in sanitising history. "The growth of a museum culture (in Britain a museum opens every three weeks, and in Japan over 500 have opened up in the last fifteen years) and a burgeoning "heritage industry" that took off in the early 1970s, add another populist (though this time very middle-class) twist to the commercialism of history and cultural forms. "Post-modernism and the heritage industry are linked," says Hewison, since "both conspire *to create a shallow screen* that intervenes between our present lives and our history." History becomes a "contemporary creation, more costume drama and re-enactment than critical discourse".[18] (emphases mine)

Fig. 4 An aerial view of the Henry Ford Museum (Courtesy of the collections of Henry Ford Museum & Greenfield Village).

The typical technical exhibit continues to favour the clean over the messy aesthetic ideal. It is a pattern that tells us how difficult it is to free our imaginations from the ideology of a benign and inevitable technological "progress", a vision wherein all victims are temporary down payments for future blessings and all critics those who fear to face the future. But what of exhibitions that articulate — in the three-dimensional idiom that renders museums an irreplaceably unique form of public discourse — the essential ambiguity of every technical endeavour, that insist on raising questions of power and exclusion, of who wins and who loses, as technological resources are allocated according to some design elite's vision of the common good? Fluency in such a symbolic vocabulary continues to elude us.

Still gatherings as this one at The Cité are hopeful signs of change. Critical discourse, on an international level, about the place of technical museums in the larger society encourages an increasingly adult approach to technical display, one where exhibits call forth critical and contemplative encounters between the ordinary citizen who walks our halls and these complex artifacts. When our visitors leave with a deeper sense of the essential humanity of the technological endeavour, aware that technological choices reflect the full range of humanity, intelligence and stupidity, nobility and venality, then museum professionals will have taken a substantial step toward influencing public discourse.

Notes

1   Stories of Ford's unpredictable interventions appear in the oral reminiscences of Edward Cutler. For example: "One morning, Mark Nied, the plasterer… came up to me and said, 'What are we going to do with this back wall. It is an inch and a half out of line.' I said, 'The simplest way to do it is to put

mud on thick in the middle.' He started putting the mud on thick in the middle, and Mr. Ford happened to come in at that time. He *always did come in when you were trying to bury something up.* He said, 'What are you doing here?' I said, 'That back wall is an inch and a half out of line. That's the simplest way I know to straighten it up.' He said, 'To hell with that! Tear the damn thing down.' We had to tear the whole back wall out, line it up, and put it back an inch and a half. That's one time I made a poor judgment." *Oral Reminiscences of Mr. Edward J. Cutler.* Interview, May-June 1951, Oral History Section, Ford Motor Company Archives, Vol 1, pp. 37-38.

2   Veteran Graham McNamee of NBC was the announcer. *A Home for Our Heritage: The Building and Growth of Greenfield Village and Henry Ford Museum, 1929-1979,* Geoffrey C. Upward, museum editor, Dearborn, MI, The Henry Ford Museum Press, 1979, p. 69.

3   The museum opened on June 22, 1933. Geoffrey Upward, *A Home for Our Heritage, op.cit.,* p. 76.

4   The transition from an antiquarian to a social history perspective at the museum and village officially began with the hiring of Harold Skramstad as director. Immediately before his arrival, Larry Lankton wrote a highly critical review which came to be known as the "sleeping giant" review. "In the museum world it remains the sleeping giant. The technological collections from the nineteenth and early twentieth centuries are superb... But the collections still await a board of trustees, an administration, a curatorial staff, and an exhibit philosophy and design that will do them justice." Larry Lankton, "Something Old, Something New: The Reexhibition of the Henry Ford Museum's Hall of Technology," *Technology and Culture* 21, 4 (October 1980), p. 613. On the changes under Skramstad's leadership, see my "The Giant Wakens: Revising Henry Ford's History Book," *Technology and Culture* 29, 1 (January 1988), pp. 118-124.

5   Otto Moog, German engineer, in Thomas P. Hughes, *American Genesis: A Century of Invention and Technological Enthusiasm. 1870-1970.* New York, Viking, 1989, p. 291 (author's translation of Otto Moog, *Drüben steht Amerika: Gedanken nach einer Ingenieurreise durch die Vereinigten Staaten.* Braunschweig, G. Westermann, 1927, p. 72 (my emphases). Hughes cites another German engineer, Franz Westermann, saying: "the most powerful and memorable experience of my life came from the visit to the Ford plants..." (p. 99).

6   *My Art, My Life,* pp. 187-88.

7   *Ibid.* Some of Rivera's more volatile Detroit critics, after the 1933 unveiling of his River Rouge murals, would have found his professed admiration for Ford incredible. Dr. George Hermann Derry, President of Marygrove College for Girls in Detroit, expressed a common emotion during the uproar. "Wake up, Mr. Edsel Ford! On the walls of the Public Education Building in Mexico City, Rivera has told the world what he thinks of your father, Mr. Henry Ford. There, in a setting of wine and women, Rivera has painted for posterity your father as a leering, luxury-loving, wine-bibbing stock gambler with one hand fondling the ticket [sic] tape, and with a champagne glass in the other, pledging the health of a young women who is not his wife. On the walls of Detroit's Art Museum, Rivera has painted your monster machines crushing the life out of the bent bodies and brutalized faces of the working men of Detroit." *Detroit Free Press,* March 24, 1933, p. 7.

8   See Stephen Meyer III, *The Five Dollar Day: Labor Management and Social Control in the Ford Motor Company, 1908-1921.* Albany, N.Y., State University of New York Press, 1981, *passim.*

9   Nevins and Hill summarise the new Ford vertical integration as follows: "...by 1926 the entire productive activity of the company had been impressively developed. Raw materials were now flowing from the iron mines and lumber mills of the Upper Peninsula, from Ford coal mines in Kentucky and West Virginia, and from Ford glass plants in Pennsylvania and Minnesota, much of the product traveling on Ford ships or over Ford-owned rails. Ford manufacture of parts had been expended — starters and generators, batteries, tires, artificial leather, cloth, and wire had been manufactured by the company in increasing quantities." *Ford: Expansion and Challenge,* p. 257, cited in T.P.Hughes, *American Genesis, op.cit.,* pp. 209-210.

10   Ford sued the *Tribune* for libel, was grilled on the stand with lines of questions demonstrating his flimsy educational background, and was awarded six cents in damages. Robert Lacey, *Ford: The Men and the Machine.* Boston, Little, Brown and Co., 1986, pp. 197-202.

11   On the stockholder buyout see Alan Nevins and Frank Ernest Hill, *Ford. Expansion and Challenge: 1915-1933.* New York, Charles Scribner's Sons, pp. 105-11. Nevins interprets the three resignations as follows: "Ford... looked aback with distaste on the period of Couzen's activity in company affairs, when he had been unable to move freely. The Dodge suit had of course intensified his desire for absolute authority. He was therefore irritated by the presence of anyone in the company who might not work with him in complete harmony." (*Ibid.* p.145)

12   "When he and his team were creating the Model T and the Ford system of production, there were no lines of authority, routine procedures, or experts. Theirs was a resourceful, ingenious, hunt-and-try probing into the unknown future... (Ford) continued to advocate a leadership style suited for times of invention and great change long after the Ford company had become an extremely large and a

relatively stable managerial and technical system with high inertia. Ford would not, or could not, make the transition in leadership style from the inventive stage to the managerial." T.P.Hughes, *American Genesis, op.cit.*, pp. 214-216.

13 Cutler, *Reminiscences*, vol. 2, p. 13.

14 Lacey, for example: "...there was only one beautiful room in the entire building: the powerhouse. This was a spare, clean chamber which Henry had designed himself... and he created a very Ritz of power stations, all marble and gleaming brass dials and pipes. Around the floor were set out little generators, raised on plinths like so many modern sculptures..." pp.149-50. See also Nevins, pp. 20-21. The clean, uncluttered, "Ford" style that Charles Sheeler would make famous with his late twenties photographs and paintings represent the *continuation of, and not a completely fresh artistic reflection* on, the Ford style. See Mary Jane Jacob, "The Rouge in 1927: Photographs and Paintings by Charles Sheeler", in *The Rouge: The Image of Industry in the Art of Charles Sheeler and Diego Rivera* (funded by the Ford Motor Company Fund and Founders Society Detroit Institute of Arts).

15 Robert O. Derrick, *Oral Reminiscences*, p. 50 (emphases mine). Cited in Upward, *A Home for Our Heritage, op.cit.,* 1979, p.50. For a discussion of the striking parallels between Ford's need to "see everybody" and utilitarian philosopher Jeremy Bentham's principle of constant scrutiny for the "Panopticon" see my "Science and Technology: Who Gets a Say?" For the Conference: "Technological Development and Science in the 19th and 20th Centuries" (Technische Universiteit Eindhoven, The Netherlands, November 1990).

16 Chicago Century of Progress International Exposition, *Official Book of the Fair*. Chicago, A Century of Progress Inc., 1932, p. 11. I am indebted to Lowell Tozer's "A Century of Progress, 1833-1933: Technology's Triumph Over Man", *American Quarterly* 4, No. 1 (Spring 1952), pp. 78-81, for first calling my attention to the Exposition and to Cynthia Read Miller, curator of photographs and prints in the archives at the Henry Ford Museum and Greenfield Village for copies of the official book and photographs of the iconography referred to below.

17 Popular feelings about technocratic elitism was clearly mixed. Industrial unions flourished in the thirties as workers organised to contest managerial high-handedness. On the other hand, even so shocking an episode as 1937's battle of the overpass evoked an outpouring of fervent support for Ford's dictatorial labour style in hundreds of handwritten letters from ordinary citizens around the country. (Archives and Library Department, Henry Ford Museum & Greenfield Village, Dearborn MI, Acc. 292 Box 43). My cursory inspection suggests that the vast majority of the letters, although not all, strongly favour Ford's position.

18 David Harvey, *The Condition of Postmodernity: An Enquiry into the Origins of Cultural Change*. Oxford, Basil Blackwell, 1989, pp. 62-63. The citation within the quote is R. Hewison, *The Heritage Industry*. London, 1987, p. 135.

CORPORATE ADVERTISING, PUBLIC RELATIONS AND POPULAR EXHIBITS: THE CASE OF DU PONT

David J. Rhees

American Philosophical Society, Philadelphia, U.S.A.

It is well-known that industrial corporations have played an active role in shaping the interpretations of science and industry purveyed by museums. Less well understood, however, are the specific economic and political interests which motivate corporations. One might assume that any corporation would wish to get its message into a museum, but I think this is the exception rather than the rule. As recent studies of popularisation have shown, scientists must be very strongly motivated before they are able to overcome professional biases against talking to the public.[1] Likewise, my research indicates that corporate involvement with museums rarely occurs without strong motivating factors. As I will show, the Du Pont Company's sponsorship of popular exhibits was prompted by several public relations crises and advertising problems. I would like to suggest that one cannot properly interpret the cultural meanings and social functions of museums of science and industry without understanding the context of corporate advertising and public relations within which industrial exhibits are constructed.

What follows, then, is a case study of the corporate politics behind the Du Pont Company's popular exhibits.[2] For the sake of brevity, I will focus on a Du Pont exhibit displayed at science museums in New York and Philadelphia during the late 1930s. Although Du Pont continued to produce hundreds of popular exhibits after World War II, the company seemed to forsake museums for other kinds of "advertising vehicles", and I will suggest some possible reasons for that trend. As an epilogue, I will turn to some recent exhibits which mark the return of Du Pont to the museum.

The Rise of Educational Advertising at Du Pont

Before discussing specific exhibits, it is useful to briefly summarise the early history of Du Pont and how various problems encountered by the company led to a new advertising philosophy. The Du Pont Company was founded along the Brandywine river in the state of Delaware in 1802 by the French immigrant Eleuthère Irénée Du Pont de Nemours. E.I. Du Pont de Nemours and Company quickly became the dominant American manufacturer of gunpowder (and dynamite and smokeless powder, later in the century) to the extent that it was accused of being a "powder trust". During the first two decades of the twentieth century, however, Du Pont transformed itself from an explosives producer into a diversified chemical manufacturer. Forced to divest some of its black powder and dynamite holdings in 1913 by a government anti-trust suit, and flush with profits made from selling explosives to the Allies during the First World War, Du Pont purchased numerous businesses in adjacent chemical areas, including paints, varnishes and cellulose plastics. It also set up a complete synthetic coal-tar dye factory, one of the first in the U.S. The research laboratories which Du Pont had established in 1902-03 became doubly important with the diversification of the company into "high tech" areas such as synthetic organic dyes, and in 1928 the company launched an ambitious programme of fundamental research which led to the invention during the 1930s of neoprene rubber, nylon, lucite and many other "wonders of chemistry".[3]

The transformation of Du Pont from a powder company into a giant, science-based chemical manufacturer was accompanied by some serious marketing and image problems. First, the public had to be convinced that new synthetic chemical products were superior to natural materials. Second, diversification created an identity problem for the company: the public still associated Du Pont with munitions and the powder trust, an image that became intolerable by the 1930s. Third, Du Pont had become one of the largest companies in the country and was an easy target for anti-big business sentiment.[4]

One of the ways in which Du Pont responded to these problems was by launching what it considered to be a new kind of advertising — "educational advertising" — in which exhibits played a prominent role. In describing a 1918 company display at the National Exposition of Chemical Industries, a recently founded trade show held in New York City, the *Du Pont Magazine* noted that "the exhibit was of interest not merely to technical men and women, but it had in it the element of education which, though apparently new in the marketing of goods, for a number of years has been the policy of the Du Pont Company".[5] In addition to educational displays for trade shows, Du Pont also prepared exhibits for schools, colleges, and even department stores. One of Du Pont's most successful educational efforts was the establishment in 1916 of a permanent company exhibit on the boardwalk in Atlantic City, New Jersey, a popular seashore resort, where products made with Du Pont materials such as cellophane, rayon, fabrikoid and pyralin plastic were displayed and explained (though explosives were rarely mentioned). By the time the Atlantic City exhibit was closed down in 1955, more than twenty-six million visitors had passed through its doors.[6] Du Pont considered these kinds of exhibits to be educational because they eschewed direct selling and provided some degree of popularised technical information. As the *Du Pont Magazine* stated, "This company believes that all products of merit warrant publicity through instruction."[7]

"Publicity through instruction" and "educational advertising" became even more important to Du Pont during the antiwar agitations of the mid-1930s, when the company once again came under public attack for its role as an explosives maker. In 1934 company officials were called before a U.S. Senate Committee headed by Gerald P. Nye that was investigating alleged profiteering by munitions makers during World War I. Although Du Pont's record was relatively clean, the company was irrevocably labelled in the public mind as a "Merchant of Death".[8]

The "Merchants of Death" debacle prompted Du Pont to hire a public relations firm — Batten, Barton, Durstine & Osborne — which planned a comprehensive programme of advertisements, radio programs, films and popular exhibits. The now famous slogan of that campaign, launched in October 1935, was "Better Things for Better Living... Through Chemistry".[9]

The "Better Things for Better Living... Through Chemistry" Exhibit

By an interesting coincidence, when Du Pont launched its "Better Things for Better Living" campaign, three new museums of science and industry had just opened in the United States: the Chicago Museum of Science and Industry, which opened in 1933; Philadelphia's Franklin Institute Science Museum, in 1934; and the New York Museum of Science and Industry, which opened in Rockefeller Center in 1936.[10] Although the specific details of their establishment varied with local conditions, these museums shared a number of traits. First of all, they had common roots in the industrial boom of the 1920s (when efforts to establish the museums were initiated) and in the widespread enthusiasm of that era for popular education in science and technology. Second, they all looked to a common source of inspiration — the great science museums of Europe, particularly the Deutsches Museum — whose "interactive" exhibit techniques they widely emulated. A third common trait was that each institution opened its doors wide to industrial corporations. Companies were asked to produce exhibits about their areas of expertise and to pay a fee for the privilege of displaying them. Although some attempt was made to limit commercialisation, the museums exercised relatively little control over corporate exhibit content. Since all these museums opened in the midst of the Depression, financial necessity may have encouraged this somewhat indiscriminate use of industrial exhibits.[11]

By coincidence, the new museums began to solicit corporate exhibits at the same time as Du Pont began looking for outlets for its new institutional advertising campaign. Thus when the New York Museum of Science and Industry invited the company to prepare an exhibit, it readily accepted. The result was a 1600 square-foot display which opened on 31 March 1937, and ran for six months before being sent to Philadelphia's Franklin Institute Science Museum for another six-month venue. The exhibit took its title directly from Du Pont's new slogan: "Better Things for Better Living... Through Chemistry."

While it is not my intent to provide a detailed exegesis of this exhibit, I would like to offer a few illustrations of how Du Pont's interpretation of the role of chemistry in American life was shaped by the three problems I noted earlier: winning consumer acceptance of synthetic materials, changing Du Pont's image from munitions to chemistry, and combating public resentment of big business.

Perhaps the dominant theme of the exhibit was the superiority of "synthetic" over natural products.[12] Demonstrations and push-button displays "proved", for instance: that cellulose sponges absorb four times as much water as natural sponges (moreover, they do not sink when left in the water, as do natural sponges); that neoprene is more resistant to attack by gasoline, oils and oxygen than natural rubber; that pyroxylin-coated fabrics such as Du Pont's fabrikoid make excellent book covers that are grease-proof, insect-proof and washable; that synthetic coal-tar dyes offer vivid, long-lasting colours never seen before in nature, at affordable prices; that plastics such as plasticele, pyralin and lucite could take on any desired colour and, "unlike any natural materials, could be molded, blown, sawed, cut, hammered, drilled, polished or carved"; and that chemically-treated fabrics could be made crease-resistant, flame-proof and water-repellent.[13]

The basic point of this litany of "better things" was that a "chemical age" had dawned in which synthesised materials were surpassing and replacing nature's own handiwork. By associating these slightly suspect synthetics, with their weird names and strange properties, with scientific progress, modernity, and of course "better living", Du Pont's exhibits sought to legitimate them. The museum itself — even a museum of science and industry — also conferred a kind of legitimation. As an institution which traditionally served as a temple or rare, if not "sacred" artifacts and antiquities, the museum "sanctified", as it were, any objects placed with its precincts, even those as secular as cellulose sponges. As the New York Museum of Science and Industry told its industrial patrons, "There can be no question of doubt as to the value of the Science Museum to industry due to its museum status."[14] The legitimating power of the museum was stretched to the limit, however, when the museum allowed Du Pont to stage a fashion show on opening night, featuring ladies clothing and accessories made with products of the chemical laboratory. Through the use of such techniques, the prestige of "Science" and the legitimating aura of the museum helped the new synthetic materials gain acceptance in the marketplace.[15]

Another major goal of Du Pont's exhibit at the New York Museum of Science and Industry was to shift the image of the company from that of a munitions maker — a "merchant of death" — to that of a chemical company. (Chemicals, of course, did not yet carry the negative connotation that they do today.) This concern was expressed, on the simplest level, by what was *not* shown in the exhibit: although Du Pont still made explosives, only their agricultural uses were mentioned, such as blowing up tree stumps. The *new* image of Du Pont, on the other hand, was expressed in practically every aspect of the exhibit: in the lecture-demonstrations given by Du Pont personnel; in the film which accompanied the exhibit, called "The Wonder World of Chemistry"; in the opening night speeches by Du Pont executives, which were broadcast on Du Pont's radio programme, "Cavalcade of America"; and of course in the exhibit title — "Better Things for Better Living… Through Chemistry." Although these messages may seem no more than the conventional scientific boosterism of the interwar era, they also fulfilled a hidden agenda: to change the company's image from munitions and death to better living and chemical progress.

"Chemistry" also provided a single image with which to unify Du Pont's expanding array of product lines. A display entitled the "Kinship of Du Pont Chemical Products" made this point with an animated electrical panel that depicted the company's diverse operations in terms of a "family tree" of chemicals. The image of chemical kinship helped convey a clear corporate identity to customers, stockholders and employees, thus enhancing sales of individual products as well as improving internal company morale.

The third important aim of the exhibit was to disarm public criticism of Du Pont as a big business. One approach to this problem was to show how Du Pont aided farmers and small businesses. One display, for instance, showed how Du Pont made fountain pen barrels and toiletware from the fuzz on cotton seeds, and antifreeze from molasses. As the Du Pont lecturer told museum visitors, "this new partnership between chemistry and agriculture means for the farmer new and growing markets for his crops, and millions of dollars in added income."[16] Other Du Pont exhibits emphasised how new industries created by Du Pont's chemical laboratories had spawned hundreds of new businesses, thereby creating new jobs. And of course, the "Better Things for Better Living" theme served this purpose by showing how the lives of average citizens were being improved by Du Pont's products.

After closing at the New York Museum of Science and Industry, the Du Pont exhibit moved to the Franklin Institute in Philadelphia where a "Rayon Salon" was added and where Franklin Institute staff replaced Du Pont advertising personnel as the lecture-demonstrators. (Perhaps there was concern that the Du Pont admen were being a little too commercial.) A total of 142,000 persons visited the exhibit in Philadelphia, at a cost, carefully calculated by Du Pont, of only 3.4 cents per person.[17]

This exhibit was only one of many produced by Du Pont, and was by no means the most ambitious. A much larger exhibit called "The Wonder World of Chemistry" was sent to regional expositions around the country during the late 1930s. Du Pont's biggest, most spectacular effort, however, was its building at the New York World's Fair in 1939-1940, which cost $ 887,000 and was seen by 9.7 million visitors.[18] Du Pont also produced a major exhibit for the 1964-65 World's Fair in New York, though neither the exhibit nor the fair itself had as great an impact as the earlier ones.

The nature of the postwar exhibits varied, of course, with local conditions as well as with general trends in public opinion. When President Harry Truman's administration launched an anti-trust suit against Du Pont in 1949, Du Pont exhibits were adjusted accordingly.[19] In 1951, Du Pont prepared an exhibit in New York's Pennsylvania Railroad Station in honor of the senventy-fifth anniversary of the founding of the American Chemical Society — the Diamond Jubilee, as it was called. This exhibit placed great emphasis on the fact that Du Pont had just invested $ 30 million in a new addition to its Experimental Station laboratories in Wilmington,

Delaware, a model of which was included in the display. At these laboratories, labels indicated, "more than 800 scientists will carry on fundamental research — looking for completely new scientific knowledge that may or may not result in commercially successful products." Lest this be considered too altruistic, the exhibit text quickly added that "This kind of research resulted in neoprene chemical rubber (1932) and nylon (1938) — products you use almost every day." Furthermore, the exhibit stated, "It takes a big industry to create the countless new products of chemical research...," and these new products in turn create new jobs.[20] The point of such rhetoric was that only very large companies like Du Pont could afford the advanced laboratory research facilities which brought society these benefits. In other words, big business makes possible big science, which in turn brings better living. Despite such variations in tone, emphasis, size and content, the basic themes of all Du Pont exhibits remained much the same well into the post-World War II period.

Popular exhibits were only one among many methods that Du Pont used to deal with its advertising and public relations problems. They seemed to be effective, however, if one can believe the anecdotal evidence of visitors' letters and interviews. Writing in 1953 about a visit to the Du Pont exhibit at Atlantic City "many years ago when I was young", Miss Mary F. Bugbee, a retired government employee from Washington, D.C., wrote, "I realized then and have never forgotten that only when a business concern has some profits which it is allowed to keep can it do research work on such a large scale, research from which the public has derived great benefit."[21] One elderly lady who visited the 1939 New York World's Fair exhibit told the lecturer that "I thought of the name Du Pont as being associated with explosives up until the time I saw this exhibit. After having gone through it, I found many wonderful things and no explosives." [22] And after visiting a Du Pont exhibition in 1949, one housewife wrote to the company that "I left the exhibit with an earnest desire to replace everything in our home, insofar as possible, with nylon or plastic."[23]

In the absence of case studies of other companies, it is not easy to assess the degree to which Du Pont was typical of general corporate involvement in museums. Certainly many companies besides Du Pont produced exhibits for museums. In 1938, for instance, the New York Museum of Science and Industry received about $35,000 in rental fees from eleven industrial exhibitors.[24] It is true, of course, that few companies had suffered from the kind of shock which Du Pont experienced during the "Merchants of Death" fiasco. Nevertheless, the 1930s was a period of extreme economic and political stress for the corporate world in general. The anti-big business sentiment that worried Du Pont worried many companies. The Great Depression obviously hurt corporate sales. And the perceived threat of the socialisation of industry by President Franklin D. Roosevelt's New Deal instilled feelings akin to paranoia in many businessmen. Indeed, the New York Museum of Science and Industry exploited these fears and worries: in a memorandum used to solicit corporate support, the museum emphasised "industry's interest in its own future well-being in a free-enterprise economy".[25] Although Du Pont may be an extreme case, the crisis conditions of the 1930s created a motivational climate that encouraged general industrial involvement in museums. During the era of postwar prosperity and conservatism, however, the climate changed.

Postwar Changes

In spite of the evident good will garnered by its popular exhibits, it seems that Du Pont placed very few of its exhibits in museums after World War II. One reason was that some of the problems of the 1930s which had motivated the original advertising campaign had eased by the late 1950s. Synthetic materials had won a permanent place in the American economy; the "Merchants of Death" label was slowly fading away; and the anti-trust suit against Du Pont was dismissed in 1954.[26] In that year, one member of the Du Pont Public Relations Department noted a "significant re-alignment of public thought" in a conservative direction. He considered this shift to be a natural outgrowth of the postwar rise in prosperity, and believed that most of the public had accepted big business as a wholesome and necessary element of society.[27] Opinion polls confirmed this trend, showing that Du Pont's "favorable" rating had risen from 47% in 1937 to 84% by 1954. [28] The postwar "return to normalcy" ushered in an era of unprecedented prosperity and public prestige for Du Pont, and hence a return to more conventional forms of marketing.

Another important factor in the shift away from corporate museum exhibits was that Du Pont found better ways for getting across its advertising and public relations messages. Trade shows, which provided an efficient way to reach a carefully targeted audience of buyers, became particularly popular with the company. The number of these trade shows had increased dramatically, rising from 900 in 1940 to over 3,000 in 1955.[29] Taking advantage of these new advertising outlets, Du Pont more than quadrupled the number of conventions at which it displayed exhibits during the decade after World War II; by 1956 these displays would reach an estimated 3.2 million business and professional men.[30] While trade shows allowed Du Pont to focus on specific audiences, mass media such as radio and television allowed the company to reach a broad, national constituency. By 1952 Du Pont's "Cavalcade of America" radio programme was reaching a total of about 4.1 million people. Du Pont also established a television version of "Cavalcade", which in 1952 reached 8.1 million people.[31] Compare these numbers with the mere 142,000 who viewed the "Better Things for Better Living... Through Chemistry" exhibit at the Franklin Institute, and one can see why the company foresook museums.[32] Like it or not, museums — even State-funded museums — are part of the media marketplace and must compete with trade shows and TV for public attention and corporate advertising dollars.

At the same time as Du Pont began to seek other advertising avenues, some museums may have relaxed their efforts to cultivate corporate support because they were able to tap new sources of government funding. Particularly after the *Sputnik* crisis in 1957, federal money for "public understanding of science" became readily available from agencies such as the National Science Foundation (N.S.F.). In the early 1960s, for instance, the N.S.F. played an active role in the establishment of two new science centres — the Lawrence Hall of Science at Berkeley, California, and the Pacific Science Center in Seattle, Washington. [33] Just as the economic crisis of the 1930s may have forced science museums into the arms of industry, postwar affluence and government largesse may have encouraged a less intimate relationship.[34]

The Response to Chemophobia

By the 1980s, however, new public relations difficulties prompted Du Pont to come back to the museum. The reputation of the chemical industry took a severe beating from negative publicity concerning pesticides, toxic chemical wastes, the use of chemical warfare agents in the Middle East, and especially the tragic accident in December 1984 at the Union Carbide plant in Bhopal, India, where some 2,000 persons died. Indeed, the Bhopal tragedy has had the same shocking effect on the entire chemical industry as the "Merchants of Death" accusations had on Du Pont in the 1930s.

The result is that chemists and the chemical industry have gone on the defensive. "Chemophobia" on the part of the American public has been widely detected and decried. As one observer recently noted, "chemist bashing has become a popular sport."[35] In about 1980 Du Pont dropped the words "Through Chemistry" from its slogan, which became simply "Better Things for Better Living".[36] The Dow Chemical Company came very close to dropping

"Chemical" from its name because of public hostility toward chemistry.[37] More recently, Du Pont's sensitivity to environmental issues prompted it to launch a daily programme on public radio called "Pulse of the Planet", which featured brief stories about nature intended to give Du Pont a "greener" public image. Many other companies and trade associations have taken steps to counter the public backlash against chemicals and the chemical industry.[38]

Such concerns about the negative public image of chemistry very likely influenced Du Pont's decision to contribute nearly one million dollars (the sole source of funding) for a major exhibition at the Smithsonian Institution's National Museum of American History, called "A Material World", which opened in 1988. More recently, Du Pont was one of the major contributors to the American Chemical Society's $35 million "Campaign for Chemistry". One of the top priorities of this campaign is to improve public understanding of chemistry, and toward this end the American Chemical Society has committed $5,5 million to the Smithsonian (the largest single grant in the Smithsonian's history) for a 12,000 square-foot exhibit on "Science in American Life". Scheduled to open in 1993, the exhibit will prominently feature the history of chemistry and other physical sciences, and will include a large interactive science-centre component.[39]

To be sure, corporate funding of these Smithsonian exhibits does not constitute a return to the 1930s situation in which companies designed and installed their own exhibits and simply rented floor space from museums. Public taste and social norms have changed over the past half century, and any hint of commercialism in a museum exhibit is usually met with swift condemnation.[40] Most companies today realise this and do not attempt to inject advertising in exhibits which they fund. Nevertheless, it seems likely (and I freely admit that my sources for these recent developments are impressionistic and incomplet) that Du Pont's return to the museum was motivated at least in part by the belief that such exhibits would help improve the tarnished public image of chemistry and the chemical industry.

Conclusion

The case of Du Pont indicates that when corporations choose to support museums of science and industry, it is usually because they have an advertising or public relations problem and need the legitimation and prestige of the museum. In the absence of a crisis, corporations may prefer to use more conventional outlets for their advertising messages, such as trade shows or the mass media. However, as long as museums require outside funding, and as long as corporations have public relations and advertising problems, the science-based industries will continue to exert an influence on the ways in which museums interpret science and industry to the public.

Notes

All manuscript citations unless otherwise noted are from the Hagley Museum and Library, Wilmington, Delaware. Collections are abbreviated as follows:
Acc. 1410, Records of E.I. du Pont de Nemours & Co., Inc., Public Affairs Department, Accession 1410 II, 2, Records of E.I. du Pont de Nemours & Co., Inc., Series II, Part 2

1   For instance, one of the goads which prompted the American chemical profession to launch a major campaign of popular education during the interwar period was the widespread public criticism of American chemists during the "dye famine" of World War I. See David J. Rhees, *The Chemists' Crusade: The Rise of an Industrial Science in Modern America, 1907-1922* (Ph.D. dissertation, University of Pennsylvania, 1987), pp. 72-77. See also Marcel C. LaFollette, *Making Science Our Own: Public Images of Science in America, 1910-1955.* Chicago, University of Chicago Press, 1990, and John C. Burnham, *How Superstition Won and Science Lost: Popularizing Science and Health in the United States.* New Brunswick, NJ, Rutger University Press, 1987 .

2   My choice of Du Pont as a case study was facilitated by the availability of the excellent archive of Du Pont Company papers at the Hagley Museum and Library in Wilmington, Delaware. I gratefully

acknowledge the support of an N.E.H.-Mellon Advanced Research Fellowship at the Hagley Library in 1990, and I would like to thank Patrick Nolan, Michael Nash, and the other members of the Hagley staff who assisted me in my research.

3   The best treatment of Du Pont's scientific and technological contributions is David A. Hounshell and John Kenly Smith, Jr., *Science and Corporate Strategy: Du Pont R & D, 1902-1980*. Cambridge, Cambridge University Press, 1988.

4   Another important political problem which concerned Du Pont from World War I to the early 1920s was the need for tariffs to protect the company's infant synthetic dye business from German competition. The use of popular chemistry exhibits and literature to build public support for dye tariffs is recounted in David J. Rhees, *The Chemists' Crusade, op.cit.*, pp. 263-330 (see ref. 1).

5   Quotation from "Reflections on Fourth National Chemical Exposition," *Du Pont Magazine* (December 1918), p. 21; David J. Rhees, "Chemistry on Display: The Early Years of the Chemical Exposition, *Today's Chemist*"(April 1990), pp. 22-26.

6   "The Du Pont Exhibit, 25 Years of Service on the Atlantic City Boardwalk..." (1941), II,2, box 11; statistic from *Atlantic City Press,* 10 October 1955, copy in box 12.

7   "Reflections on Fourth National Chemical Exposition," *Du Pont Magazine* (December 1918), p. 21.

8   In addition to extensive newspaper publicity, Du Pont was featured in *Merchants of Death: A Study of the International Armament Industry,* by Helmuth C. Englebrecht and Frank C. Hanighen, which became a best-seller. John E. Wiltz, *In Search of Peace: The Senate Munitions Inquiry, 1934-36.* Louisiana State University Press, 1963.

9   The philosophy of the campaign was outlined in Bruce Barton to Lammot du Pont, 18 May 1935, Acc. 1662, box 3, "Advertising Dept., July 1932 - Dec. 1935" file.

10   As John Staudenmaier notes in his paper (*supra*) the Henry Ford Museum in Dearborn, Michigan, was opened to the public in 1933. However, it was more of a proprietary or company-type museum and thus rather different in form and function from the institutions in Chicago, Philadelphia and New York.

11   A brief overview of the development of museums of science and industry is in Victor J. Danilov, *Science and Technology Centers*. Cambridge, MA, MIT Press, 1982, pp. 22-28. An unsuccessful attempt during the 1920s to found a National Museum of Engineering and Industry is documented in Arthur P. Molella, "The Museum That Never Was: Anticipations of the Smithsonian's Museum of History and Technology," *Technology and Culture* 32, 2 (April 1991), pp. 237-263. By 1939, guidelines for industrial exhibitors had been drawn up at the New York Museum of Science and Industry which specified limits on the size of the company's name and logo; nevertheless, exhibit content was still left primarily in the company's hands. See "Exhibition Requirements," ca. 21 December 1939, Rockefeller Foundation archives, RG1.1, series 200R, box 262, folder 3120, Rockefeller Archive Center. On the Industrial Participation Program instituted in 1940 by Lenox R. Lohr, president of the Chicago Museum of Science and Industry, see James G. Mann, "Theater of American Capitalism: Chicago's Museum of Science and Industry, 1940-1968," unpublished paper, 1987.

12   Strictly speaking, "synthetic" materials are man-made, non-natural, off-the-shelf chemicals. In popular parlance, however, any substance that involved extensive chemical processing, even if utilising natural products (such as celluloid, made from chemically-treated plant fibres), was loosely referred to as synthetic.

13   Unless otherwise noted, my discussion of the "Better Things for Better Living... Through Chemistry" exhibit is based on the following sources: "Some Recent Products of the Diversified Chemical Manufacturing Industry as Represented by Du Pont Which Are Having Important Effects on Industry, Shown at the New York Museum of Science and Industry, Beginning March 31, 1937" (*Du Pont News Bulletin*), and F. J. Byrne, form letter to the editors, 26 March 1937, both in George W. Gray Collection, box 80, "Ersatz" folder, Rare Book and Manuscript Library, Butler Library, Columbia University. See also Edward J. Pechin, "At Rockefeller Center...," *Du Pont Magazine* (June 1937) p. 8; "Now at Philadelphia," *Du Pont Magazine* (November 1937), p. 24. Publicity photographs of the exhibit are in the Hagley Museum and Library Pictorial Collections, e.g., 72.341.39. The quotation is from Du Pont Style Service, "Memorandum on Du Pont Exhibition at the New York Museum of Science and Industry," 30 March 1937, Acc. 1410, box 44, see also the other news releases in Acc. 1410, box 44.

14   Memo attached to Frank B. Jewett to Arthur W. Packard, 7 July 1941, Rockefeller Foundation archives, RG2, Cultural, box 20, folder 196, Rockefeller Archive Center.

15   Of course, legitimation can flow both ways: in the generally materialistic culture of interwar America, industry legitimated science (and museums of science) by showing that abstract scientific ideas eventually lead to concrete, useful, and profitable products.

16   "Lecture for Du Pont Exhibit, Franklin Institute," (1937), Acc. 1410, box 61-A, "Stine, C.M.A." file.

17   "History of Du Pont Exhibits, 1935-1945," p. 76, Acc. 1410, box 58. After its Philadelphia venue, "Better

Things for Better Living... Through Chemistry" ended its career at Du Pont's Atlantic City Exhibit.

18   "History of Du Pont Exhibits, 1935-1945," Acc. 1410, box 58, p. 123.

19   Du Pont's postwar antitrust problems are recounted in L.L.L. Golden, *Only by Public Consent: America's Corporations Search for Favorable Opinion*. New York, Hawthorne Books, 1968, pp. 301-317.

20   J.S. Hukill to D. Mortellito and W.H. Uffelman, 10 July 1951, II, 2, box 32. On the A.C.S. Diamond Jubilee, see Charles A. Browne and Mary E. Weeks, *A History of the American Chemical Society: 75 Eventful Years*. Washington, DC, American Chemical Society, 1952, chapt. 20.

21   In J.S. Hukill, "Report on Company Exhibits Activities in 1952," 6 March 1953, II,2, box 59.

22   John Bovco, in "Lecturers' Reports - July 15, 1939, Shift B," II,2,box 35.

23   Mrs. Winfred Jones to Du Pont Co., 12 Sept. 1949, "Visitor Comments" file, II,2, box 60.

24   "Report on Activities of the New York Museum of Science and Industry from January 1, 1938 through December 31, 1938," pp. 4-5, Rockefeller Foundation archives, RG1.1, series 200, box 262, folder 3118, Rockefeller Archive Center.

25   Memorandum, p. 4, attached to Frank B. Jewett to Frederic B. Platt, 2 July 1941, Rockefeller Foundation archives, RG2, box 20, folder 196, Rockefeller Archive Center.

26   It is true that the antitrust case was appealed by the Government and that the Supreme Court ruled in 1961 that Du Pont must divest its sixty-three million shares of General Motors stock. Even so, Du Pont was cleared of the original conspiracy charges and it was able to obtain legislative tax relief for its shareholders upon sale of the G.M. stock. L.L.L. Golden, *Only by Public Consent*, pp. 309-317 (see ref. 19).

27   C.M. Hackett to Harold Brayman, 29 October 1954, Acc. 1410, box 42, "Public Relations" file.

28   Wm. A. Hart, "Ideas In Du Pont Advertising," 26 May 1955, Du Pont Advertising Clinic talk, II, 2, box 18.

29   L.T. Alexander, "How to Get the Most Out of Your Exhibits Section," 30 Oct. 1956, II, 2, box 60, "Speeches and Articles (1)" file.

30   The number rose from 41 shows in 1946 to 180 shows in 1955. William H. Uffelman, "1947 Exhibits Section Activities", Jan. 1948, II, 2, box 60, "Reports" file.

31   W.A. Hart, "Welcome and Opening Remarks," 31st Advertising Clinic, May 28, 1953, II, 2, box 18.

32   It should be noted that Du Pont did not entirely withdraw from supporting museums in the postwar period. In 1952, in celebration of Du Pont's 150th anniversary, the company founded a museum and library on the grounds of its original powder works along the Brandywine river near Wilmington, Delaware. The Hagley Museum and Library is not a company museum, in the traditional sense, since it is administered by an independent foundation and has become a leading center for the study and exhibition of American industrial and technological history in general. From a public relations viewpoint, the Hagley Museum has functioned rather like the "Cavalcade of America" radio program, that is, its exhibits serve to associate Du Pont with themes of American progress and patriotism. Its audience, however, has been limited for the most part to local Du Pont employees and Delaware residents.

33   Bruce V. Lewenstein, *Public Understanding of Science in America, 1945-1965* (Ph.D. dissertation, University of Pennsylvania, 1987), p. 312.

34   A 1979 report on science museums concluded that the museums of the Smithsonian Institution have been less swayed by corporate influence than science and technology centres because they have enjoyed generous federal support. Howard Learner, *White Paper on Science Museums*. Washington, DC, Center for Science in the Public Interest, 1979, p.48.

35   W. Alfred Mukatis, "Chemical Sensitivity" (letter to the ed.), *Chemical & Engineering News* (4 June 1990), p. 66-67.

36   The motivation for dropping "chemistry" from the slogan is not clear. One chemist who worked for Du Pont at the time claimed that "the real reason was that chemistry had become a four-letter word." Gordon H. Schnaper, "Chemistry's Good Name," *Chemical & Engineering News* (21 May 1990), p. 82. However, an official of the company who was involved in the decision told me that the public image of chemistry had nothing to do with it; rather, it was because Du Pont had diversified to the point that it was no longer a chemical company.

37   "Dow and Chemical Like Love, Marriage Belong Together," *Wall Street Journal* (23 January 1989), p. B-9.

38   See, for example, "Chemical Firms Press Campaigns to Dispel Their 'Bad Guy' Image," *Wall Street Journal* (20 September 1988), p. 1.

39   Ernest Carpenter, "Multimillion-dollar Fund Drive Launched by ACS," *Chemical and Engineering News* (14 March 1988), p. 28; *Science in American Life: A Feasibility Study*. Washington, DC, National Museum of American History, June 1989, p. 34.

40   See Learner, *White Paper on Science Museums, op.cit.*, (ref. 34).

CELEBRATION OR EDUCATION? THE GOALS OF THE U.S. NATIONAL AIR AND SPACE MUSEUM

Alex Roland

Duke University, Durham, N.C., U.S.A.

The U.S. National Air and Space Museum (N.A.S.M.) plans to refurbish and display the *Enola Gay*, the airplane that dropped the atomic bomb on Hiroshima at the end of World War II. This historic aircraft has been in the possession of the Smithsonian Institution, N.A.S.M.'s parent organisation, since 1949. During most of those years, it was stored in pieces at a remote warehouse outside Washington, D.C. The decision to restore the artifact and put it on display in the popular Air and Space Museum has set off a storm of controversy.

The meaning of this artifact is in the eye of the beholder. Some see it as an instrument of unprecedented destruction, an object of shame and horror that blights, or ought to blight, the national conscience. Others see it as a tool of retribution, which avenged the atrocity of Pearl Harbor and shortened the war in the Pacific, saving untold American lives. Perceptions of the artifact itself are further shaped by perceptions of the museum. Some see N.A.S.M., and indeed all the museums of the Smithsonian Institution, as halls of fame, monuments to American achievement and glory. Others see them as educational centres, where all artifacts of historical significance, be they good or bad, inspiring or dismaying, should be put on display for their heuristic value. For some, then, exhibiting the *Enola Gay* seems to be a celebration of America's most inhumane act. Others see it as a powerful history lesson that can help all visitors to the museum come to grips with what they think about strategic bombing, nuclear weapons, and the mass destruction made possible by modern science and technology. The former want the *Enola Gay* left in the closet; the latter want it on display with the other great heirlooms of American aerospace history. The controversy sheds light on American concepts of museums and technology, and the proper relation between the two.

To prepare the public for exhibition of the *Enola Gay*, the National Air and Space Museum has sponsored a fifteen month series of lectures, seminars and workshops. To them have been invited the world's leading authorities on strategic bombing — scholars, participants and public officials. In them has been aired the widest possible variety of views and arguments, both pro and con. The proceedings are now being gathered in an edited volume which is likely to become the most comprehensive and authoritative book on strategic bombardment ever produced, not excluding the famous U.S. Strategic Bombing Survey published after World War II. N.A.S.M. will not change the minds of the strongest advocates in this debate, but it will at least make clear that it has given voice to every possible persuasion. These proceedings will be the reservoir from which the exhibit script for the *Enola Gay* display will be drawn.

Without anticipating how that script will finally read, and without engaging in an evaluation of the merits or demerits of the Hiroshima bombing in particular or strategic bombing in general, it is nonetheless possible to gain some insight into this debate by examining the history of the Air and Space Museum itself. Part of this debate turns on the purposes of the museum, whether it is meant to celebrate or simply to display historically significant artifacts for their educational value.

A clear answer to that question should inform any decision about displaying the *Enola Gay*.

The history of the N.A.S.M. and of the artifacts it displays is deeply rooted in the history of the Smithsonian Institution. This unique public entity is the result of a bequest to the United States from James Smithson (1765-1829), a British scientist of modest achievement and great inherited wealth. His bequest specified that the money support "an establishment for the increase and diffusion of knowledge among men" (and presumably women). It further stipulated that the United States would be trustee "for purposes not limited to the national interest but on behalf of all mankind".[1] His intent was clearly education, not celebration of national achievement.

The intent of Congress was less clear. Some congressmen did not even want the money, seeing it as condescending charity from British aristocracy. Having finally decided to accept the gift, Congress spent years trying to decide what to do with it.[2] They needn't have bothered. In practice it has been the successive secretaries of the Smithsonian, with the advice and consent of a board of regents, who have largely shaped the institution. By promoting congressional support for their activities, they have supplemented the original Smithson bequest with annual appropriations that now make up by far the largest part of the operating budget.

Not the least of these secretaries was Samuel Pierpont Langley, a distinguished astronomer and astrophysicist who headed the institution from 1887 until his death in 1906. Among his many contributions to the growth of the institution, he created the National Zoological Park, still one of only a few zoos devoted to both research and public exhibition. Here he studied the flight of birds and converted that knowledge into the quest for human flight. Having succeeded in flying a small, unmanned, heavier-than-air vehicle in 1896, Langley accepted a grant from the army when the Spanish-American war broke out to build a manned aircraft for military

Fig. 1 The Langley Laboratory, behind the famous castle building of the Smithsonian Institution. (Courtesy of N.A.S.M.)

observation and communication. In a small structure behind the famous Smithsonian Castle, Langley designed and built a flying machine. Twice he launched it from a platform in the Potomac river and twice it fell ignominiously in the drink. The second fiasco, in December 1903, conducted in view of sceptical reporters, brought hoots of derision and public caricature of Langley as a "professor wandering in his dreams".[3] Langley retired from the enterprise, a humiliated and discredited pioneer, and died barely two years later.

Within two weeks of his humiliation, however, two bicycle mechanics from Dayton, Ohio, attained what the great scientist and his substantial resources could not. Wilbur and Orville Wright achieved heavier-than-air flight at Kitty Hawk, North Carolina, on 17 December 1903, changing the course of history and, furthermore, setting in chain a strange and unpleasant series of events that would ultimately result in the creation of the N.A.S.M. Before that came to be, however, their once cordial relationship with the Smithsonian Institution would turn bitter and destructive.

When the Wrights had decided to investigate heavier-than-air flight, they turned first to the leading centre of scientific and technical knowledge in the United States, the Smithsonian Institution.[4] Wilbur wrote directly to Secretary Langley, who sent back to the young and unknown correspondent by return mail a whole package of literature on flying. The Wrights always gave great credit to Langley and the Smithsonian for helping them early in their adventure, and they lamented the sorry end to which Langley's researches finally came. The Smithsonian Institution was all along the logical home for the historic Wright *Flyer* of 1903 in which they made their first flights, and the plane surely would have gone there when retired but for the intervention of a bitter and drawn-out dispute over patent rights and prior art.

From 1903 to 1908, the Wrights struggled to establish in the eyes of the world the significance of what they had achieved. Thereafter they spent much of their time defending their patents against those who came to recognise and then appropriate their achievement. At the heart of the Wright system was wing-warping, a means by which an aircraft could be controlled in roll, that is, movement about its longitudinal axis. The courts uniformly sided with the Wrights in ruling that roll control was fundamental to flight and that the Wrights had developed the means to achieve it. All other would-be flyers, then, at least in the United States, had to pay the Wrights a royalty for the use of their patented idea.

Among those who tried to break the patent was Glenn Curtiss, a brilliant inventor, mechanic and entrepreneur who in fact improved upon wing-warping with his own system of ailerons, the method still used on most aircraft. Still, the Wright patent would not yield to even this substantial but nonetheless incremental improvement on the Wright invention. With the aid of Alexander Graham Bell, a regent of the Smithsonian Institution, and Charles D. Walcott, Langley's successor as Smithsonian secretary, Curtiss took the 1903 Langley aerodrome to his research facility in Hammondsport, New York, redesigned it, and flew it successfully in an attempt to demonstrate prior art. The demonstration failed to convince the courts, but it did alienate Orville Wright, not just from Curtiss and his associates, but from the Smithsonian Institution as well. In Wright's eyes, the Smithsonian had lent itself to this perfidy in an attempt to salvage the reputation of Langley, a perception that was not entirely erroneous. After his brother's untimely death in 1912, Orville spent the remainder of his life protecting their claims to precedence in the achievement of manned flight. He would brook no challenges to their historic priority. Nor would he forgive the Smithsonian for the role it played in the Curtiss gambit. The Langley aerodrome had been seriously altered by Curtiss, and until the Smithsonian publicly admitted this, Orville Wright would not allow his 1903 *Flyer* to reside in the Smithsonian Institution. Instead, he sent it to the Science Museum of London in 1925, explaining to a distressed correspondent: "I believe that my course in sending our Kitty Hawk machine to a foreign museum is the only way of correcting the history of the flying machine, which by false and misleading statements has been perverted by the Smithsonian Institution. In its campaign to discredit others in the flying art, the Smithsonian has issued scores of… false and misleading statements. They can be proved to be false and misleading from documents. But the people of today do not take the trouble to examine the evidence. With this machine in any American museum the national pride would be satisfied; nothing further would be done and the Smithsonian would continue its propaganda. In a foreign museum this machine will be a constant reminder of the reasons for its being there, and after the people and petty jealousies of this day are gone, the historians of the future may examine the evidence impartially and make history accord with it."[5] In other words, the Wright *Flyer* of 1903 was sent to London as a way of pressuring the Smithsonian.

The *Flyer* remained in London until after Orville's death in 1948. Long before that, however, Orville made provision for the plane to return to the U.S. and be displayed in the Smithsonian. A will signed in 1937 provided for the return of the *Flyer* upon condition that the Smithsonian set the record straight. Soon thereafter, Fred C. Kelly, a reporter, writer and long-time friend of Orville Wright who was working on an authorised biography of the brothers, undertook to settle the dispute with the Smithsonian. He convinced Smithsonian secretary Charles G. Abbot to publish a detailed account of the technical differences between the Langley aerodrome of 1903 and the Curtiss reconstruction that flew at Hammondsport in 1914. The account appeared in the *Smithsonian Miscellaneous Collections* on 24 October 1942, preceded by a notification that Orville Wright had read and approved the statement in advance of its publication. Dr. Abbot concluded the Smithsonian's public apology with the following observation: "If the publication of this paper should clear the way for Dr. Wright to bring back to America the Kitty Hawk machine to which all the world awards first place, it will be a source of profound and enduring gratification to his countrymen everywhere. Should he decide to deposit the plane in the United States National Museum, it would be given the highest place of honor, which is its due."[6]

The following year, Orville wrote to the Science Museum in London saying that he would request the return of the 1903 *Flyer* after the end of World War II. He additionally drafted a new will, never signed, which said "I give and bequeath to the U.S. National Museum of Washington, D.C., for exhibition in the National Capital only, the Wright aeroplane (now in the Science Museum, London, England) which flew at Kitty Hawk, North Carolina, on the 17th of December 1903."[7] The way was cleared for the Smithsonian Institution to display the most treasured artifact of human flight. All it needed was an appropriate home.

The impetus to create such a home came from the military. World War II had stirred in its participants a keen sense of history and an appreciation of the momentous event that had just passed. Most wanted to capture that history for posterity, and to save its artifacts as well. Chief of the U.S. Army Air Forces Henry H. Arnold was especially anxious to preserve examples of the U.S. aircraft that had flown in the war. He began a collection of such planes and worked in Washington to create a museum to house them. Arnold himself preferred to develop an air museum in one of the wartime aircraft manufacturing plants then being sold as surplus, but he found himself drawn instead into a plan by the military to run a museum housed within the Smithsonian Institution. When this plan went to Congress, it was divided in two. One part supported creation of a national air museum in the Smithsonian; the other looked to the creation of a national military museum elsewhere.[8]

Thus, patriotism and appreciation for the role of the military in World War II influenced Congress as it came to consider legislation authorising creation of a national air museum. But paramount in everyone's mind was the centrality of the Wright *Flyer*. The House report on the proposed legislation called for "a complete history of the airplane, starting with the first Wright airplane and carrying through every other type of airplane both commercial and military".[9]

When General Arnold testified in favour of the bill, he said that Orville Wright, an old friend who had taught him to fly, could be approached to return the original *Flyer*.[10] One suspects that he knew Wright had already made arrangements to return the plane. There was a movement to include a statue of American air pioneer Billy Mitchell in the museum, but it was the Wright *Flyer* that was clearly to be the centrepiece.

The legislation signed into law by President Truman on 12 August 1946 said that the purpose of the museum was to "memorialize the national development of aviation; collect, preserve, and display aeronautical equipment of historical interest and significance; serve as a repository for scientific equipment and data pertaining to the development of aviation; and provide educational material for the historical study of aviation".[11]

These same purposes, later amended to include spaceflight, remain the mission of the NA.S.M. The first and last of these purposes were the same ones observers were still arguing about forty-five years later when trying to decide on exhibiting the *Enola Gay*. The real question was which of these four missions, if any, was the real purpose of the museum and which if any were simply good reasons for creating such an institution.

A hint at the answer was provided years later when Harold Miller, co-executor of the Orville Wright estate, wrote to Senator Barry Goldwater to say that the estate had agreed to the return of the 1903 *Flyer* "in the confident expectation that there would be a second-to-none U.S. Air Museum in which it would be the premier Exhibit, displayed in a setting appropriate to its unique character and merit like the crown jewels".[12] In the view of the Wright executors, the purpose of the museum was to memorialise — especially the Wright *Flyer*. That clue, however, was revealed in the summer of 1971, during the final stages of the fight for construction of a museum. This was a quarter of a century after the initial legislation. In the story of that delay is embedded the answer to the question of what purpose the museum was meant to serve, education or celebration.

The United States Congress distinguishes between authorisation and appropriation. Authorising legislation originates in committees that focus on given functions of government; in the case of the National Air Museum Act of 1946, it was the Committee on the Library. Authorising bills are relatively easy to pass, because congressmen are loath to frustrate the pet projects of their colleagues. Appropriation of the funds to actually carry out the authorised activity is a different matter. This legislation comes down from the powerful Appropriations Committee, where the many demands on the federal treasury must be queued up in order of priority. Here the popular legislation to create a National Air Museum ran afoul of other more pressing business. No appropriation was passed to support the authorised construction. Rather the Smithsonian was directed to identify suitable lands and buildings for the museum and recommend these to Congress. There began a drawn-out process that took years to complete.

While the Smithsonian searched and the Congress deliberated, the nation's aeronautical artifacts were collected in Washington and a small number were actually placed on display. The Wright *Flyer*, for example, was returned from England in 1948 and exhibited in the Arts and Industry Building behind the Smithsonian Castle. A former Douglas Aircraft plant at Orchard Park (now O'Hare) Airport just outside Chicago was made available for storage in the same year. It soon became the repository of the large collection of Army Air Force's planes pulled together by General H.H. Arnold. This collection, including the *Enola Gay*, was transferred on paper to the National Air Museum in 1949, but the aircraft remained in Illinois for want of proper facilities in Washington. When the Douglas plant was reactivated during the Korean War, the Smithsonian had to find new storage facilities. It finally acquired an appropriate site at Silver Hill, Maryland, just outside Washington, where many of the Smithsonian's aerospace artifacts and much of its restoration work remain housed today. Meanwhile a surplus World

Fig. 2 The "*Tin Shed*", a World War I aviation building made available to the Smithsonian Institution. It was erected on the site of the old Langley Laboratory. The top of the Smithsonian Castle is visible over the building. The Arts and Industry Building, where the Wright *Flyer* was first displayed, is visible at the far right. (Courtesy of N.A.S.M.)

War I aviation building, which had been erected behind the Smithsonian Castle in 1917 on the site of the original Langley Laboratory, was made available to the institution. The so-called "*Tin Shed*" served for many years as the Air Museum anticipated in the 1946 legislation[13] With the Wright *Flyer* once more in the United States, the sense of urgency that had marked passage of the original bill seemed to abate. Not even the Smithsonian ranked the air museum as its highest building priority.[14]

The mid-1950s witnessed a concerted effort to approve a building for the Air Museum, spurred in part by the interest in the fiftieth anniversary of the Wright brothers' first flight.[15] The secretary reported to Congress in 1954 that a gift from the "Aircraft Association and the Air Transport Association" had funded the preparation of "preliminary studies for a suitable building to house the Wright brothers' Kitty Hawk *Flyer*, Lindbergh's *Spirit of St. Louis*, America's first supersonic jet plane (the X-1), and all the other great planes and aeronautical equipment that make up the Smithsonian's world-famous and unique collection".[16]

The rhetoric through the mid-1950s remained similar to that which had won passage of the Air Museum Act in 1946: aviation was a peculiarly American achievement and the Wright *Flyer* was the great artifact. As Smithsonian Secretary Leonard Carmichael reported in 1955: "The airplane is in many respects the product of the genius of the American people. The Smithsonian collections in this great field, begining with the Wright brothers' 'Kitty Hawk' itself, are unrivaled in the world."[17]

After a failed effort in 1956 to reserve a site across Independence Avenue from the Smithsonian Castle, Senator Clinton P. Anderson of New Mexico introduced legislation in 1957 to reserve the plot of land on the Mall that now houses the N.A.S.M.[18] At first the only congressional opposition to this proposal focused on the cost of the museum building that would follow.[19] Soon, however, this campaign ran afoul of the artistic community in the United States. Long anxious to create a national centre for the performing arts, the community launched a major campaign to win for its own purposes the choice piece of land approved for the Air Museum. Its argument was that the arts should be centrally housed in Washington, while an air museum would be more suitably located at an airport or some other remote and spacious site. The battle between "arias and airplanes",[20] as one observer described it, raged through 1958 to the advantage of neither group. Each would eventually have its way, the artistic community finally achieving the Kennedy Center for the Performing Arts in Foggy Bottom and the air enthusiasts finally holding the site already selected on the Mall. But the conflict delayed completion of both projects for years.

In their attempt to save the Air Museum from the artistic community, the aviation enthusiasts elevated their rhetoric several octaves and rehearsed the motives that really lay behind creating such an institution. Smithsonian Secretary Leonard Carmichael told the Senate Committee on Public Buildings that such a museum would be a "monument to aviation" and a "shrine for the Wright plane" and others. "Aviation," he continued, "is peculiarly an achievement of American science and of American inventive genius."[21] Jimmy Doolittle, pioneer aviator and hero of World War II, echoed Secretary Carmichael's views, arguing that "the Wright brothers' plane... deserves a shrine," in part, he continued, to inspire America's youth. "Airmindedness is to be encouraged," he told the Senators; "the first step toward an aeronautical career is the wish to participate in this profession which has a great past and an unlimited future". "The National Air Museum," he continued, "is intended to be a lasting memorial to America's unique record in the air."[22] To the previous arguments about enshrining national artifacts, especially the Wright *Flyer*, was now added a dimension of education. But it was education of a specific sort, a kind of civic education that would inspire youth to careers in aviation and remind all Americans of their rich heritage.

Chauvinism was just around the corner. Grover Loening, an American aeronautical pioneer of no mean achievement himself, told the same committee that the Wright *Flyer*, "the greatest relic of that kind in the world," should be displayed in "a glass-enclosed dome," for it represents "a kind of genius that has never been equaled by any other nation." The museum, he concluded, would serve "notice to the other nations of the world that America leads in the air now and always has, since the original invention of mankind's wings." He explicitly linked two of the most frequently used terms in the debate when he advised "The Air Museum would be more than a building just to house an aircraft collection. It would principally be a memorial to enshrine the greatest mechanical relic in the world — the first airplane to fly."[23]

In the minds of at least some supporters, the term "memorialise" in the original legislation clearly meant "enshrine". Education of a chauvinistic and civic variety was part of the enterprise as well, but the primary purpose for the Air Museum was to be a house of worship: America was the religion, Orville and Wilbur Wright were the most visible saints, and the 1903 *Flyer* was the true cross.

Sidelined by the conflict over siting, the Air Museum entered the 1960s with its building still a dream. Indeed it was not until the mid-1960s that serious progress resumed. By then, the context of these developments had changed significantly. For one thing, S. Dillon Ripley had succeeded Leonard Carmichael as secretary of the Smithsonian. An ornithologist and patrician lured to the Washington post from the directorship of the Peabody Museum of Natural History at Yale University, Ripley was to serve twenty years as secretary and reshape the Smithsonian as perhaps no other secretary. During his tenure the Smithsonian added eight new museums and seven new research or support facilities, and the number of visitors more than doubled. He was, as one reporter approvingly concluded, "the great aggrandizer in Smithsonian history."[24] The emphasis in his aggrandisement was clearly on art, with the opening of the National Portrait Gallery, the National Museum of American Art, the Hirshhorn and the Renwick Gallery, and the acquisition of the Cooper-Hewitt Museum in New York and the Museum of African Art. [25] No one ever mistook Dillon Ripley for having a particular affection for the Air and Space Museum, but he nonetheless pursued this project actively and did what he could to bring it to fruition.

His one major reform of the plans for the museum was to insist that it focus on education and scholarship. Even before coming to the Smithsonian, he had believed that "museums must establish themselves as essential educational institutions", which to his mind entailed a significant research component. [26] This persuasion seems to have influenced his choice of a new director for the Air Museum. S. Paul Johnston, who took the post in 1965, embraced Ripley's view of the importance of research and education. When Johnston drafted his first set of "proposed objectives and plans" for the museum in January 1965, he devoted one of the longest sections to "education and research".[27] The new dispensation was that the museum should be "educational as well as inspirational".[28] Ripley even enlisted his assistant secretary for history and art, directing him to "give some thought to the research and education program of the new... Museum." The air museum represented, he continued, "a magnificent opportunity to demonstrate the scholarly potential of museums."[29] Ripley's reading of the original 1946 provision to "provide educational material for the historical study of aviation" went far beyond what the drafters of the legislation seem to have had in mind. It nonetheless became an indelible part of the museum's mission and the campaign to fund a building.

The other major change shaping the renewed campaign to win an appropriation for the museum was the emergence of an American space programme. After the shock of *Sputnik* in 1957 and the creation of N.A.S.A. the following year, the United States slowly began to grow competitive with the Soviet Union. Alan Shepard became the first American to fly in space in 1961; John Glenn the first American to orbit the Earth the following year. When their Mercury spacecraft, *Freedom 7* and *Friendship 7* respectively, were donated to the Smithsonian, attendance at the National Air Museum exploded. In 1963, 2,674,000 visitors converged on the *"Tin Shed"* and the single gallery in the Arts and Industry Building where the air and space artifacts were on display. These numbers led quickly to projections that five million people a year would visit the museum when it was built, adding yet another argument to the list that would be paraded before Congress in the coming years.[30]

In January 1964 the Smithsonian Regents recommended that the name of the proposed museum be changed to the "National Air and Space Museum." Representative Clarence Cannon introduced such a bill in the House in February, Clinton P. Anderson in the Senate in March; both men were Smithsonian regents [31] Curiously, both bills asked not only to change the name of the museum but also to reauthorise construction. The 1946 legislation clearly authorised construction, even though no funds had ever been appropriated. But the Smithsonian wanted the issue clarified in order that planning funds could be sought in 1965 and actual construction funds appropriated in 1966.

Congress failed to complete action on this bill in 1964. When it was reintroduced in 1965, it died in the powerful Senate Committee on Rules and Administration. On the third try, in 1966, the legislation was finally passed and became Public Law 89-509. Once more, however, the Committee on Rules and Administration intervened. It directed that "appropriations should not be requested, unless and until there is a substantial reduction in our military expenditures in Vietnam."

The restriction on appropriations was maddening, for there seemed no way to know when the conditions might be met. The Smithsonian asked to have the appropriation request inserted in the president's budget in 1968, 1969 and 1970, only to be denied.[32] Nerves began to fray.

S. Paul Johnston, who had been appointed director of the Air Museum in anticipation of overseeing construction of the new building, began to despair of achieving his goal. He came to blame Dillon Ripley and the senior management of the Smithsonian for the delays, but the records at the Smithsonian suggest that matters were truly out of their hands. It seemed that nothing could break the log-jam.

The landing of *Apollo 11* on the moon in July 1969 changed everything. As early as June 1967, Eugene M. Emme, the N.A.S.A. historian, had written to Dillon Ripley enjoining him to exploit the coming moon landing to get the Air and Space Museum appropriation.[33] Closer to the event, a staff member of the Smithsonian wrote to Deputy Secretary Sidney R. Galler that "not since the Mona Lisa and the Dead Sea Scrolls came to town has there been a public relations potential" to match the possibility of displaying a moon rock after the first Apollo mission.[34] The Smithsonian moved quickly both to congratulate N.A.S.A. after the historic landing in July and to secure the first moon rock to go on public display. The result was predictable and spectacular. More than 200,000 visitors viewed the moon rock during its first month on display at the Smithsonian.[35] Down the road lay the prospect of exhibiting the *Apollo 11* command module that had actually travelled to the moon. Here was an artifact comparable in splendour and appeal to the Wright *Flyer*. Surely this was the most propitious moment since the return of the Kitty Hawk plane in 1948 to secure funding for a new building.

When Dillon Ripley was invited by President Nixon to attend a dinner in California honouring the *Apollo 11* astronauts, he took advantage of the occasion to work the chief executive: "Now, if ever, the American people need a reminder of our aviation and space history and accomplishments: a living monument which honors and promotes that sense of adventure you have so eloquently described as 'The Spirit of Apollo'. It seems the ideal place, a showcase on the Nation's Mall, for the recent accomplishments of N.A.S.A. as well as the unique history of America's technological breakthroughs in air and space."[36]

Behind the scenes Dillon Ripley and the Smithsonian staff lined up all the political support they could muster for a formal campaign to include construction funds in the president's 1971 budget. In the process, they invented new justifications for the museum at a dizzying pace. In addition to the twin rationales of inspiration and education that had become hallmarks of the Ripley administration, the staff added the growing popularity of the topic and the international interest in the Apollo moon rocks. In drafting a rationale for Congress in 1969, Frank A. Taylor, director general of museums at the Smithsonian, told Ripley: "My pitch is to the things that Congress reacts to — crowds of people and the image of the United States." [37] Dillon Ripley drafted a letter for congressman Frank Bow to send to Nixon advisers saying that the museum would be "an ornament to his administration."[38] They even employed a little Cold War leverage, bringing to the attention of a White House staffer news that the Russians were planning a space museum.[39]

The campaign culminated in the meeting of the Smithsonian Board of Regents on November 5, 1969, where a new plan for an air and space museum was approved just four months after the moon landing. When Chief Justice Warren Burger, chairman of the Board of Regents, reported their action to the president, he cited "the tremendous surge of interest among all Americans engendered by the historic flight of *Apollo 11*." He went on to extol "this great education and exhibition center which will show the Nation and the world our ability to develop technological skill and to perfect inventive engineering for the benefit of all mankind." Except for the last phrase, which was lifted from the wording of the plaque left on the moon, this statement had much of the civic pride of previous arguments but without the chauvinistic rhetoric.

Still, this was not enough. John D. Ehrlichman, assistant to the President for Domestic Affairs, informed Dillon Ripley on 20 January that military expenditure in Vietnam had not yet declined sufficiently to allow the new request in the 1971 budget. On the same day, another White House aide wrote to Smithsonian Regent William A. Burden, declining his request for an audience with the president on the subject of the Air and Space Museum. Not even the Apollo moon landing, it seemed, could get the Air and Space Museum approved.

It took Barry Goldwater. The conservative Republican senator from Arizona, who had left the Senate in 1964 to make his failed run for the presidency, returned in 1969 to resume the politics for which he had become justly famous. On 19 May 1970 he rose on the floor of the Senate to address a "Time of Crisis for the National Air and Space Museum." Taking his cue from S. Paul Johnston, the retired and disaffected director of the Air and Space Museum, Goldwater laid the blame for the building's delay at the feet of Dillon Ripley, senior Smithsonian officials, and the Board of Regents. Arguing that the Air and Space Museum had not been receiving resources and attention commensurate with its importance and with public demand, Goldwater concluded a long oration by calling for immediate funding of the museum building: "Now that this landmark in the history of mankind [the Apollo landing on the moon] has occurred and public excitement about space achievements has catapulted, I believe the time has arrived when the American people want to have a decent home for the national center where the world's greatest collection of aircraft and space objects can be shown. Americans want to have a center where they can enjoy the incomparable inspirational feeling which their heritage in flight and space can offer. In these troubled times, the people want to have some resources where they can gain a feeling of pride in human accomplishment."[40]

Whatever clever rationales might have been cooking at the Smithsonian, Senator Goldwater went back to basics. His argument was for good, old-fashioned celebration of American achievement. This was enshrinement, pure and simple.

Fig. 3 The completed National Air and Space Museum, on the site selected for it in the 1950s. It did not open its doors until July 1976. (Courtesy of N.A.S.M.)

Fig. 4 The main foyer of the National Air and Space Museum, with the 1903 Wright *Flyer* in the central position that was always intended for it. (Courtesy of N.A.S.M.)

Goldwater continued his crusade through 1970, culminating in a personal interview with the president in February 1971 and still more oratory on the floor of the Senate in April of that year. In that speech and others he called on Congress to live "up to the promise given to the memory of Orville and Wilbur Wright." [41] Finally the White House relented and allowed funds to be included in the 1972 Smithsonian budget to redesign the air and space museum. The step moved Dillon Ripley to hazard the prediction that "if the schedule presently outlined can be achieved without let or hindrance from act of God, strikes, fires, or flood, we are in a fair way to have a National Air and Space Museum within five years, namely by 1976."[42] *Apollo 11* astronaut Michael Collins accepted appointment as director of the museum in the same year the redesign was approved, and his "captivating enthusiasm", as Ripley put it, together with his enormous prestige, helped to win passage of the appropriation bill the following year. Construction began on 11 September 1972.

As Ripley had predicted, the building opened to the public 1 July 1976, within days of the two hundredth anniversary of the signing of the Declaration of Independence. One million visitors were counted in the first month, a rate that has hardly diminished in the ensuing fifteen years. As its advocates had suggested and its supporters still claim, it is the most visited museum in the world, a testament to the public interest in flight and its artifacts. Those crowds will surely not be diminished if the *Enola Gay,* another unique and moving relic, is added to the collection currently on display.

But can it be put on exhibit without celebrating its 1945 mission? The history of the Air and Space Museum provides grist for the mills on both sides of the debate. The move for an air museum really began with General Hap Arnold immediately after World War II; *Enola Gay* was one of the aircraft he collected for the purpose. The public rhetoric, however, quickly came to focus on the Wright Brothers, the Kitty Hawk *Flyer*, and the enshrinement of American aviation firsts. There was talk of education, but this was mostly of a civic and chauvinistic variety, still in the realm of inspiration.

S. Dillon Ripley put his mark on the museum by insisting that it have a true educational and research component. Not himself personally interested in aerospace matters, Ripley wanted the museum to serve some purpose beyond mere celebration of machines. Even his considerable skills at empire building, however, were not sufficient to move Congress to appropriate the necessary construction funds. Ripley and his staff tried every imaginable argument from the vast public enthusiasm for spaceflight to the vanity of the president and finally even the threat of being beaten by the Russians. Nothing worked.

Only when Barry Goldwater took up the old banner of celebrating American achievement did the issue finally get resolved. Education and public interest and all the rest played a role, but first and last the National Air and Space Museum was approved by Congress to celebrate the Wright Brothers, the *Apollo 11* moon landing, the *Spirit of St. Louis*, and the other great firsts of American aerospace achievement. It remains to be seen if the staff of the Air and Space Museum can overcome this history and make the exhibit of the *Enola Gay* the educational opportunity it is planning. Can it make this shrine into a school?

Notes

1   Quoted in James A. Steed, "Smithsonian Institution," in *Government Agencies,* ed. by Donald R. Whitnah. Westport, CT, Greenwood Press, 1983, p. 488
2   Paul H. Oehser, *The Smithsonian Institution,* Praeger Library of U.S. Government Departments and Agencies. New York, Praeger, 1970, chap. 1.
3   Tom D. Crouch, *A Dream of Wings: Americans and the Airplance, 1875-1905.* New York, Norton, 1981, pp. 126-56, 255-91. Quote on p. 291.
4   *Idem, The Bishop's Boys: A Life of Wilbur and Orville Wright.* New York, Norton, 1989.
5   *Ibid.,* p. 491.
6   C.G. Abbot, "The 1914 Tests of the Langley 'Aerodrome'," *Smithsonian Miscellaneous Collections,* Vol. 103, No. 108, 24 Oct. 1942; reprinted in *Annual Report of the Board of Regents of the Smithsonian Institution (hereafter Smithsonian Annual Report), 1942.* Washington, Smithsonian Institution, 1943, pp. 111-118; quote on p. 118.
7   Crouch, *The Bishop's Boys, op.cit.,* p. 520.
8   *Congressional Record,* 79th Cong., 2d. Sess., Vol. 92, Part 8, 31 July 1946, p. 10546.
9   U.S. Congress, House, Committee on the Library, Report No. 2473, "Establishing a National Air Museum," 79th Cong., 2d. Sess., 9 July 1946, p.1.
10   He also said that the collection should include all types right up through the latest, the B-29. The *Enola Gay* is a B-29.
11   Public Law 722, 79th Cong., 2d. Sess., 12 Aug. 1946; 60 Stat. 955.
12   *Congressional Record,* 92d Cong., 1st Sess., Vol. 117, Part 9, 26 April 1971, p. 11887.
13   Donald S. Lopez to author, 4 April 1991; *Smithsonian Annual Report, 1946.* Washington, Smithsonian Institution, 1947, p. 12.
14   The Smithsonian annual report for 1956, for example, cited expansion of the Natural History Museum as its "highest priority." *Smithsonian Annual Report, 1956.* Washington, Smithsonian Institution, 1957, p. 2.
15   *Smithsonian Annual Report, 1953.* Washington, Smithsonian Institution, 1954, p. 126.
16   *Smithsonian Annual Report, 1954.* Washington, Smithsonian Institution, 1955, p.3.
17   *Smithsonian Annual Report, 1955.* Washington, Smithsonian Institution, 1955, p.3.
18   *Smithsonian Annual Report, 1957.* Washington, Smithsonian Institution, 1958, p. 111.
19   See, for example, *Congressional Record,* 85th Cong., 2d Sess., Vol. 104, Part 10, p. 13105.
20   *Washington Post,* 16 April 1958, quoted in United States Congress, Senate, Committee on Public Works, *Hearings,* 22-23 April, p. 37. Hereafter cited as 1958 *Hearings.*
21   *1958 Hearings,* p. 37.
22   *Ibid.,* p. 39.
23   *Ibid.,* pp. 41-43.
24   Benjamin Forgey, "Ripley's Believe It & Build: Shaping Washington & the Smithsonian,"

Washington Post, 15 Sept. 1984, pp. C1 ff.
25 Edward Parks, "Secretary S. Dillon Ripley Retires after Twenty Years of Innovation", *Smithsonian* (Sept. 1984), pp. 77-86.
26 S. Dillon Ripley, *The Sacred Grove: Essays on Museums.* New York, Simon and Schuster, 1969, p. 86.
27 S. Paul Johnston, "Proposed Objectives and Plans for the National Air and Space Museum," 15 Jan. 1965, SI Archives, Record Unit 99, Box 58.
28 *Ibid.,* p. 5. See also S. Paul Johnston, "Education and Inspiration: The National Air and Space Museum," *Aerospace* (Spring 1965). The idea, of course, was not entirely original. The *Smithsonian Annual Report, 1956* (Washington: Smithsonian Institution, 1957), for example, had mentioned the "educational and inspirational function" of the National Air Museum (p. 102). But it was Ripley who gave real prominence to this purpose.
29 Memorandum, S. Dillon Ripley to Mr. (Charles E.) Blitzer, 5 Oct. 1966, Smithsonian Institution Archives (hereafter SI Archives), Record Unit 99, Box 58.
30 U.S. Congress, Senate, Committee on Rules and Administration, Subcommittee on the Smithsonian Institution, *Smithsonian Institution (National Air and Space Museum),* Hearings, 22 June 1964, p. 15.
31 S.I. Archives, Record Unit 99, Box 58, folder "NASM Advisory Board"; U.S. Congress, House, 79th Cong., 2d Sess., Report 1232, "National Air Museum Amendments Act of 1964," 22 July 1964.
32 S. Dillon Ripley to Jerome C. Hunsaker, 26 Jan. 1967, S.I. Archives, Record Unit 99, Box 57.
33 Eugene M. Emme to Dillon Ripley, 26 June 1967, S.I. Archives, Record Unit 99, Box 306.
34 R.S. Cowan to Sidney R. Galler, 30 June 1969, S.I. Archives, Record Unit 99, Box 306.
35 W.W. Warner to Dr. Ripley, Memorandum, "Love That Moon Rock!" 18 Sept. 1969; and S. Dillon Ripley to T.O. Paine, 21 Oct. 1969; both in S.I. Archives, Record Unit 99, Box 306. Warner also reported that sales in the museum shop almost tripled in the same period.
36 S. Dillon Ripley to The President, 22 August 1969, S.I. Archives, Record Unit 99, Box 306. On an earlier draft of this letter, one of the staff members at the Smithsonian wrote "I would suggest putting in the phrase 'the spirit of Apollo', somewhere, since it is a Nixon favorite these days". In a separate memorandum on the same date, Sidney Galler wrote to Ripley, "You might also wish to remark on the unique opportunity the National Air and Space Museum will provide to demonstrate to the public the transfer of knowledge from space program technology to realms of concern to society in general."
37 Frank A. Taylor to S. Dillon Ripley, 17 October 1969, S.I. Archives, Record Unit 99, Box 306.
38 S. Dillon Ripley to Frank T. Bow, 24 October 1969, S.I. Archives, Record Unit 99, Box 306.
39 Sidney R. Galler, to Jerome B. Wolff, 12 November 1969, S.I. Archives, Record Unit 99, Box 306.
40 *Congressional Record,* 91st Cong., 2d Sess., Vol. 116, Part 12, 22 July 1970, p. 16095.
41 *Congressional Record,* 92d. Cong., 1st Sess., Vol. 117, Part 9, 26 April 1971, p. 11886.
42 *Smithsonian Annual Report, 1971.* Washington, Smithsonian Institution, 1972, p. 4.

THE NEW GENERATION OF MUSEUMS:
TECHNICAL, INDUSTRIAL AND "ECOMUSEUMS"

Louis Bergeron

Ecole des hautes études en sciences sociales, Paris, France

In 1892, Colonel Laussedat, who had succeeded General Arthur-Jules Morin as director of the Conservatoire national des arts et métiers (C.N.A.M.) after the General's death in 1880,[1] received a visit from Jules Siegfried, shortly before the latter began his brief period of office in the Ministry of Commerce and Industry (December 1892 - March 1893). Siegfried had come to ask Laussedat whether it might be possible to find room in the galleries of the Conservatoire for a "Museum of Social Economy", which would house various collections assembled at the time of the Universal Exhibition of 1889. Siegfried was concerned that they should not be lost or dispersed.

An article by Laussedat in the periodical *L'Eclair* of 14 March 1893 gives an account of the interview:[2] "I said that it was not possible, for space was so short that I sometimes had to decline the offer of machinery or instruments for lack of anywhere to put them. I pointed out, however, that the church [3] might be able to house the collection."

Clearly, the C.N.A.M. museum was suffering from the very problem which today necessitates the addition of an annex or store to the Museum of Technical and Industrial History in Saint-Denis. As early as 1851, General Morin, engaged at that time on the drafting of an inventory of 28,616 models and machines, had bemoaned the fact that he did not have adequate finance or staff to properly administer the collection.

Created to house one example of every new machine, which could then be demonstrated to visiting industrialists, the museum found it impossible, after a few decades, to keep up with the explosive development of scientific and technical innovation and the rapid obsolescence of new products. The administrative breakdown which ensued led to the questioning, not only of the capability of a scientific and technical museum of such encyclopaedic capacity to overcome the practical problems of lack of space and facilities, but also of the validity of such an institution in the first place.

Of course people quote the success of the South Kensington Museum in London or the Deutsches Museum in Munich, both of which were established almost a century later than the C.N.A.M., but against that must be set the apparent failure of countries such as Spain and Italy to establish encyclopaedic museums of scientific and technical history any more capable of keeping pace with the flood of technical innovation and production than was the Paris museum.

The plastic arts present similar problems: despite the huge dimensions envisaged for the Grand Louvre of the future, it is not intended to be an all-embracing, universal museum of painting. Instead, its operations will be decentralised into an increasing number of highly specialised satellite museums.

In the past, museums have always been seen as institutions combining the functions of collective display with that of teaching and research. The C.N.A.M. museum breaks with this tradition. Although the museum benefitted from the addition of a well-stocked library, which seemed the ideal complement to its work in the field of technical history, the Conservatoire has become a powerful centre for advanced scientific, technical and professional training, and generally turns an indifferent eye to the relatively inert museum with which it cohabits, apart from coveting its storage space. That is not to say that the survival and modernisation of the museum are not eminently desirable: its historic and patrimonial importance is too great for it simply to be abandoned to its fate. But the concept it represents — that of a museum of technical and industrial history (whether eclectic or specialised) preoccupied with the collection of instruments or machines — is undeniably defunct.

Attempts to formulate a more modern, broader concept have taken people in various directions. Some authorities have placed increasing emphasis on production methods, inspired by the work, several decades earlier, of Bertrand Gille; others have concentrated on the history of industrial labour; elsewhere, pride of place has been given to the product and its evolution as a function of technological development. But whether one is dealing with production methods or the resources that such production provides, the museum should be a living example of the links between technical development and social progress.

It is increasingly desirable for an exhibition centre to be linked with other facilities, particularly libraries and archives, so that a museum should also be a place where people can study. Looked at from this point of view, the venerable Musée national d'histoire des techniques based in the C.N.A.M. could well benefit from a restructuring of the resources already to hand, but the authorities do not seem to be heading in that direction.

In order to tackle the problem of assembling under one roof the products of an endlessly developing technology, there is a tendency to rely increasingly on audio-visual reproductions of cumbersome materials and equipment such as those used in steel production, car manufacture, and the chemical or paper industries, rather than present the objects themselves. Although avoiding the difficulties of surveillance and security, this method, too, has its risks and drawbacks.

Another approach is to maintain machines and other objects, if not *in situ* (only rarely possible), then at least in areas and institutions where their preservation is less expensive, given all the prerequisites of security, durability and accessibility. I have in mind here, not a French project, but one being promoted by the Unione Industriale of Turin.[4]

One of the most interesting aspects of this scheme is that, right from the earliest stages of planning, the museum has been given an active role in the establishment of databases, and in the identification and photographing of all machinery and equipment dating from before the First World War, whether they are still in active use (in which case the business concerned is alerted to the risks of ill-conceived destruction), or are to be found in public or private collections. As well as being used as a basis for research, this inventory of "technological strata" will be useful to the future Industry Museum in Piedmont in identifying particularly significant areas that need to be brought to the public's attention.

Although the area of Piedmont has been of considerable importance in the development of the modern Italian economy, it does not possess all the resources necessary for the establishment of a national museum of technology such as is found in other countries. The use of the administrative buildings of the former FIAT factory at Lingotto would help to solve this problem.

In France, the renaissance of museology which began two decades ago has been based on an entirely different approach, that of the "ecomuseum". This covers industrial history and the cultural background of labour, but as elements of a larger entity, that of the total cultural heritage of an area which lends it its local and regional identity. In the words of the Ecomuseum Charter: "The ecomuseum is a cultural institution, depending heavily on the participation of the local population, in which research and conservation are always combined with the promotion of public awareness of the natural and cultural heritage which characterises the locality and its successive life styles."

The fact that, of the twenty-six museums of this kind which currently exist in France, the majority are situated in natural milieux or based on certain aspects of rural life, owes much to the defence of popular crafts and traditions begun forty years ago by the ethnologist Georges-Henri Rivière.

The ecomuseum at Le Creuso, established in 1973 on one of France's most prestigious sites of nineteenth century industry, seemed set to become a shrine of the new industrial museology. However, despite absorbing the library of the Society of Civil Engineers (transferred from Paris); despite the immediate proximity of a magnificent collection of industrial archives (those of the Schneider Company), and despite being on a site which boasts two centuries of industrial history, the "grafting" of the ecomuseum on to the locality has not been a complete success. And yet this western part of the Saône-et-Loire region, with its numerous industrial sites (mining and metallurgical mainly) cried out for the establishment of a huge "dispersed" museum (along the lines of what Bruno Corti calls a *museo-sistema*,[5] parts of which whould be stiuated at Montceau-les-Mines, at Blanzy, at Epinac, and along the whole length of the industrial complex bordering the Central Canal.[6]

As we enter the last decade of the twentieth century, it is the ecomuseum in the Fourmies-Trélon region, with its H.Q. in Fourmies itself, which has become firmly established as the touchstone by which other such museums are judged. One of its major successes is the Museum of Textiles and Social Life in Fourmies, which is housed in the carefully preserved buildings of the former Prouvost-Masurel woollen mill (dating from 1874) and which contains a collection of working machines unique in France. Another is the Glass Workshop/Museum at Trélon, which is housed in a glass-works dating from 1823. Here, the whole process of glass working is demonstrated, with the aid of a large collection of perfectly preserved furnaces. Recently, this system has been extended to include a broad depiction of life and work in the small region of Avesnois. Even the pilgrimages that have taken place there are represented. And yet one feels that such a system is not the ideal vehicle for industrial museology.

Fortunately, the flexibility of the French legal system with regard to associations allows for the launching of widely differing initiatives. In the course of the eighties, technical/industrial museums began to appear which were closely linked to a site — a factor which allows for a more in-depth treatment of the subject. As an extension of this, various sites falling within the same technical sector can be linked to form a "route" or "itinerary" designed to appeal both to the interested layman and the professional.[7]

The formula of the "dispersed" museum may also be applied to the industrial activities of considerably larger regions which possess their own cultural identity and history.[8] The Association for the Protection and Promotion of the Buffon Forges (in the Côte d'Or) is an excellent example of this. One of the striking aspects of its development has been the successful cooperation between former employees of the neighbouring *ecomuseum* at Le Creusot, who brought their practical experience with them to Buffon, and highly skilled researchers in technical and industrial history, steeped in the latest thinking on industrial archaeology. With the wholehearted encouragement of the current owners of the site, and with constant reference to the results of excavations and archival research, the association has progressively restored the buildings and production line to the point where the public can appreciate the operation of what was at one time a major wood-fuelled ironworks.

The site caters for a wide range of interests. In 1988 it was visited by an international scientific symposium on the occasion of the bicentenary of the death of the Comte de Buffon, a famous European intellectual who also possessed entrepreneurial abilities — it was he who established on his property in Burgundy the Great Forge which today bears his name. In addition to being listed as a historical monument in 1985 and standing on a site which has been listed since 1945, the Great Forge is a classic element of our architectural and environmental heritage, and as such attracts a wide range of ordinary members of the public. Buffon represents a successful application of the cultural synthesis (towards which we must be constantly striving) which totally rejects the ridiculous sectarian opposition between the two aspects of our heritage — traditional and industrial. This is what explains its appeal to the ordinary person on the one hand and to scientists and technicians on the other. It attracts school trips from far and wide, as well as visits by highly specialised experts and interested members of the local populace. The Buffon association has successfully linked fundamental research with the promotion of technical culture, something which all museums open to the public at large should try to emulate. At the same time it is progressively building up a "Museum of the Iron and Steel Industry in Northern Burgundy", by linking the history of Buffon with that of other neighbouring sites, including the Abbey of Fontenay.[9]

Before we leave the subject of the iron industry and metallurgy, at least one other, more recent, initiative should be mentioned: that of the Iron Mines in Lorraine, at Neufchef and Aumetz (Moselle). The sites combine to present the two techniques that were used in mining this field: the open gallery into the side of a hill, and the propped shaft. There is also a museum of working-class life, in which all technical and social aspects of mining are covered, from 1840 to the present day. Architectural and mechanical restoration begun in 1989 has greatly enhanced the authenticity of the display. The preservation of the area's heritage, in the broadest sense of the term, is successfully integrated into a general historical perspective.

But should we have to depend completely on the active members of the associative movement to ensure that research and museology combine to preserve all subsisting elements of our technical and industrial heritage? One might well think that the successors of those who created this heritage, i.e., the owners and managers of industry, would be equally interested in such a venture.

In the U.S., during the twenties, the engineers who were striving to promote the idea of a great National Technical Museum complained bitterly that American industrialists preferred to finance art galleries.[10] Their claim seemed to be contradicted by the fact that Henry Ford was then in the process of founding the museum at Dearborn (Michigan) which bears his name: between the exhibition halls and the artificial village of Greenfield, there was to be an "indoor-outdoor" museum, designed to illustrate the evolution of America from a rural civilisation to a technical, industrial society. But this type of museum was dominated by the cult of objects or machines which were in some way spectacular or exceptional, and obsessed with the establishment of collections, the criteria for which were often ill-defined, certainly in so far as they concerned the public.

In contemporary France the "entrepreneurial" museum does exist, but it rarely transcends the level of collection-exhibition. In general, industrialists do not consider that safeguarding and promoting industrial culture is up to them. Moreover they have only a limited and short-term idea of the links that their firms should strive to maintain with the environment and its history.[11] For an illustration of this, one need only think back to the incident which occurred around 1980, when the multinational firm B.S.N. decided, after minimal discussion, to destroy the "Pottery Room" at Boussois (one of the cradles of the glass industry in France), which would have provided an ideal milieu for the demonstration of ancient techniques of glass making. This contrasts with the approach that led Corning Glass Works (Corning, N.Y.) to establish a glass museum and an archive centre which today command visits from experts in the history of glass the world over.

In France, the business world has still to understand that in the field of human activity everything is culture. In this respect, industry is particularly guilty: the term "enterprise culture" has been debased to the point where it signifies little more than a set of formulae used internally to characterise social relationships within the work place, and externally, as another term for the aggression which is part and parcel of the battle for markets.

An even graver problem than the obsolescence of sites and architecture is what is happening to industrial equipment. This is sold off to the Third World or to the big metal merchants who supply certain steelworks, to the extent that it is often difficult to reconstitute materials in the logical order required by traditional technical museology.

Another administrative problem that must be addressed is that of the relationship between the associative movement and the culture it is defending on the one hand, and the State and local authorities on the other. The latter, whether at municipal, departmental or regional level, are best placed to appreciate and support associations dedicated to the promotion of technical culture, because they understand the economic benefits likely to accrue from the activites of such bodies.[12]

As for the State, that is the central administration of the Ministry of Culture and its various regional offices, its attitude to those museums which form part of the associative movement and which are involved in the protection of technical culture and the industrial patrimony, remains ambiguous. At the bottom of the administrative pyramid, one finds innovation, boldness, the readiness to take risks. From the top comes the negative influence of petty rules and regulations, backed up by the ability to accord finance or personnel, and to authorise the establishment or conservation of collections. The needs of the associative movement are in a constant state of flux, but there are times when it depends completely on public intervention. Sometimes this comes at just the right moment to allow the movement to consolidate and extend. On the other hand, in the administration of culture, the desire to make everyone toe the line and obey regulations (however dubious the benefits of the latter), coupled with the oppressive weight of institutions, traditions and outdated intellectual training, threaten constantly to block progress and hinder necessary change. In many cases there is a serious danger that the iron hand of the ministry may shatter the delicate vessel of spontaneous creation. Incomplete understanding and a willingness to resurrect out-dated traditions are too commonly evident. The tender plant of technical culture in France is still too delicate to be neglected.

Notes

1   Cf. Claudine Fontanon, "Un ingénieur militaire au service de l'industrialisation: Arthur-Jules Morin (1795-1880)", in *Le moteur hydraulique en France au xixe siècle: concepteurs, inventeurs et constructeurs*. Cahiers d'Histoire et de Philosophie des Sciences, no. 29, 1990.
2   This quotation was kindly furnished by Janet Horne, University of Virginia, Charlottesville.
3   Laussedat was referring to the Abbey of Saint Martin-des-Champs, where the Conservatoire is housed.
4   Information kindly furnished by Dr Pier Luigi Bassignana, Archivo Storico Amma (Associazione Industriali Metallurgici Meccanici Affini), Torino.
5   Cf. *Atti della giornata di Archaeologia Industriale. La memoria dell'impresa*, Torino-Lingotto 30 November 1990, Quaderni Il coltello di Delfo, Roma, 1991. Also noteworthy: Bruno Corti, "*Cinque anni di archeologia industriale*", pp. 20-21.
6   Cf. Pierre François, *Itinéraires industriels*. Ecomuseum, Le Creusot, 1982.
7   *Route des forges et des mines en Bourgogne*, edited by the Association régionale pour la promotion de l'action culturelle scientifique, Office de la culture de Beaune, 1987.
8   Project proposed by Jean-Yves Andrieux, senior lecturer at the University of Rennes.
9   Serge Benoît, *La grande forge de Buffon. Historique et guide de visite*. Buffon, 1990.
10   Charles de Lartigue, "*Les origines du National Museum of American History*", unpublished article (1989).
11   Cf. the surprising observations made at the time of the "Histoire et stratégie" symposium, Hautes Etudes Commerciales, Jouy-en-Josas, 28 Mars 1990.
12   In Haute Alsace (département du Haut-Rhin), the municipal council of the town of Mulhouse, the Conseil Général and the C.E.S.T.I.M. vigorously supported the development of the Alsace *ecomuseum* at Ungersheim and a plan to restructure all the technical museums in Mulhouse (Cloth Printing Museum, Wallpaper Museum, Railway Museum, Motor Vehicle Museum).

Abstracts

Science, Education and Museums in Britain, 1870-1914

Mari Williams

This paper reviews discussions of the roles of museums in Britain in the provision of scientific education, and as centres of entertainment during the late nineteenth and early twentieth centuries. It traces the establishment of the Science Museum and the Natural History Museum in South Kensington, and compares the arguments surrounding these major national collections with those which punctuated the development of provincial museums. In each case the paper concludes that financial and political considerations pervaded debates over the most appropriate role for a museum, and that these debates remain unresolved to this day.

Cet article examine les débats sur la place des musées en Grande Bretagne, dans l'appareil d'éducation scientifique et comme centres de divertissement à la fin du xixe et au début du xxe siècles. Il retrace l'histoire de l'édification du *Science Museum* et du *Natural Historical Museum* à South Kensington et compare les discussions qui ont entouré la mise en place de collections avec celles qui ont accompagné le développement des musées de province. L'étude conclut que, de part et d'autre, des considérations financières et politiques ont dominé les débats concernant la fonction exacte des musées, débat qui reste entier à ce jour.

A Political History of the Establishment of Museums of Technology in Modern Germany

Wolfhard Weber

In Germany, the 1960s and '70s saw the birth not only of two quite distinct though closely-related cultural ideals, but of two different kinds of technology museum. In cases where politically conservative Länder governments enjoying close ties with industrial interests decided to found museums of technology, they established institutions which presented industrial technology in a generally favourable light. In Länder governed by the social-dematrates, former factories were often used to display the region's industrial heritage, while more or less determined efforts were made to involve the general public in the planning of new museums.

However, from the early 1980s onwards, a more self-consciously "national" orientation on the part of the Bonn government led to the establishment of two huge museums whose purpose was to project a powerful image of the new Germany and enhance the prestige of the Federal Republic on the 50th anniversary of its foundation. One, in Bonn, was devoted to the founding years of the new state; the other, in West Berlin, took up the larger theme of Germany in Europe, and was in some sense intended as a rejoinder to the Museum of German History in East Berlin. Both these new museums routinely sought to present social, economic and technological themes in their political contexts. Nevertheless, these elements were employed more or less indifferently in support of essentially political statements, rather than being allowed to suggest any more profound reflections on the desirability of unchecked technical progress and the continued pursuit of economic growth. National politics thus caught up again with technology.

En Allemagne, au cours de la période suivant la Seconde Guerre mondiale, sont nés dans les années 1960 et 1970 non seulement deux concepts culturels intimement liés, mais aussi deux types différents de musées techniques. Quand les gouvernements de *Länder* — conservateurs et proches des milieux industriels — décidaient de fonder un musée technique, ils édifiaient des structures qui abritaient des présentations positives de la technique industrielle. Dans les *Länder* sous gouvernement social-démocrate, on se servait plutôt d'anciennes usines pour mettre en valeur l'héritage de la culture industrielle et l'on cherchait à donner une place, dans la création, à la participation démocratique. Une orientation plus nationale du gouvernement de Bonn conduisit cependant, dès le début des années 1980, à la fondation de musées historiques géants qui avaient pour mission de délivrer une image significative et convaincante de l'Allemagne occidentale, à l'occasion de son cinquantenaire. L'un, à Bonn, se consacrait aux premières années de la jeune République; l'autre, à Berlin, adoptait une vision plus globale de l'Allemagne en Europe et fournissait en quelque sorte une réplique inversée au musée d'histoire allemande de Berlin-Est. L'un et l'autre intégraient désormais les composantes sociales, économiques et techniques dans leur contexte politique; toutefois, ces composantes constituaient davantage des éléments interchangeables au service d'affirmations politiques qu'ils ne suggéraient des interrogations plus vastes sur la finalité profonde de l'usage d'une technique hypertrophiée et de l'aspiration à la croissance. La politique nationale a ainsi rattrapé la technique.

The Henry Ford Museum and Greenfield Village: Interwar Technocratic Idealism in the United States

J. M. Staudenmaier, S.j.

The Henry Ford Museum and Greenfield Village complex represent, in their original inter-war configuration, the convergence of a private, even solipsistic, and idiosyncratic creation of a mythic past and the public showcase of a world famous and mythic technocratic hero. Henry Ford operated simultaneously in both realms and both aspects have things to teach us. I will pay particular attention to the following: Ford's rich-man interest in collecting exotic artifacts and a profile of the kinds of artifact that attracted him; Ford's use of Henry Ford Museum-Greenfield Village as an exclusive private retreat for himself and selected friends; an overview of the resulting complex where the museum can be understood as a celebration of sterilised and inevitable progress while the village can be seen as shrines to Henry's heros; the celebration of the 50th anniversary of light, October 1929, as a national mythic event and an intensely personal act of worship. I will also try to situate these observations in the larger context of the technocratic aesthetic in the United States in the early depression years, calling on Charles Sheeler's photographs and portraits of the River Rouge Plant in the late twenties, Diego Rivera's 1933 Detroit Institute of Art murals, and the 1934 Chicago Century of Progress Exposition in particular.

Le Musée Henry Ford et le complexe de Greenfield Village dans leur configuration de l'entre-deux-guerres symbolisent la convergence entre la création personnelle, solipsiste, idiosyncratique, d'un passé mythique et la vitrine publique d'un héros universel et légendaire de la technocratie. Henry Ford jouait sur ces deux aspects, ils ont chacun quelque chose à nous apprendre. L'article insiste sur les points suivants: l'intérêt de Ford — homme fortuné — pour les collections d'artéfacts et le genre d'objets qu'il affectionnait; son utilisation du complexe comme retraite très privée pour lui-même et ses proches; une vue d'ensemble du complexe dans laquelle le Musée peut être compris comme instrument de célébration d'un progrès inévitable et stérilisé — et le village comme un reliquaire pour les héros d'Henry; la commémoration du 50ᵉ anniversaire de la lumière électrique (octobre 1929), à la fois comme événement historique national et comme acte profond et personnel de vénération. On essaiera en outre de replacer ces observations dans le contexte plus large de l'esthétique technologique des premières années de la Dépression aux Etats-Unis, esthétique que rappellent les photos et portraits de Charles Sheeler à l'usine de la rivière Rouge, les fresques de Diego Rivera dans le Detroit Art Institute, de 1933, et l'exposition universelle de Chicago, "A Century of Progress", en 1933-1934.

The City as a Museum of Technology

Miriam Levin

This paper focusses on the proposals of a coterie of civil servants, intellectuals and radical republican politicians to turn public spaces into contemporary museums for the people. Through the agency of universal expositions and lithographed posters advertising new technologies and pasted on city walls and fences, they sought to educate large and diverse segments of the population to identify these innovations with the benefits of life in a liberal democracy. But the fact that posters had become subject to the competitive conditions of the market place discouraged supporters from trying to win the French populace to accept progres in this way. They proposed that posters be collected and exhibited in a special building designated as a public museum, a space whose design and access could be controlled and where images printed on older technology could be preserved. This shift in emphasis from the concern with promoting technology through orchestration of the environment to the preservation of posters as artifacts of lithographic design signaled reformers' retreat from a belief in the possibility of using technological displays on so vast a scale to control the shape of social interactions in capitalist society. At the same time, it signaled support for a more specialised display of technological artifacts as the product of human ingenuity and skill.

L'article étudie le projet d'une coterie de fonctionnaires, d'intellectuels et de politiciens républicains libéraux consistant à transformer les espaces publics en musée contemporain pour l'édification des masses populaires. A travers l'agencement d'expositions universelles et de lithographies en couleur exposées sur les murs de la ville et mettant en exergue les technologies nouvelles, ils cherchaient à éduquer des segments larges et diversifiés de la population, les amenant à associer ces innovations aux bénéfices qu'engendre une démocratie de type libéral. Mais les affiches eurent à affronter les conditions concurrentielles du marché et leurs promoteurs se découragèrent, pour finalement abandonner l'idée de faire accepter le progrès à la population par ce moyen; ils optèrent alors pour la collecte et l'exposition des affiches dans un bâtiment spécifique construit sur le modèle du musée, un espace dont la configuration et l'accès puissent être soumis à un contrôle et où pourraient être préservées des images de technologies plus anciennes. Ce passage de la promotion de la technique à travers l'organisation contrôlée de l'environement à la préservation des affiches témoignant de l'art lithographique est signe chez les reformateurs de l'abandon de cette croyance qui veut qu'on puisse utiliser les expositions technologiques pour contrôler la forme des interactions sociales dans la société capitaliste. En même temps, c'est le signe d'une spécialisation des expositions d'objets techniques en tant que produit du génie et de l'adresse de l'homme.

An Olympic Stadium of Technology : Deutsches Museum and Sweden's Tekniska Museet

Svante Lindqvist

Sweden's Tekniska Museet in Stockholm was founded in 1924 and was to a large extent modeled after the Deutsches Museum in Munich. It was, however, more nationalistic in its aim and scope, and the paper argues that the idea of formal non-military national competition was an invention of industrial society, as manifested in the international exhibitions and the Olympic Games. The paper relates the early history of Tekniska Museet, especially the role of its first Director Torsten Althin (1897-1982) and the need for the Society of Swedish Engineers to find a symbol in their strive for social recognition. Drawing on the writings of the Swedish human geographer Torsten Hägerstrand (b. 1916), the paper introduces three dichotomies: international / national, contextual / sequential, archaeocentric / contempocentric. It argues that any museum of technology can be described in terms of these conceptuals choices.

Le musée suédois de la technique à Stockholm fut fondé en 1924, dans une large mesure sur le modèle du Deutsches Museum de Munich. Il était cependant plus nationaliste dans ses objectifs et son champ d'action, et on postule ici que l'idée qu'une compétition officielle internationale, non militaire, est une invention de la société industrielle, qui se manifeste également dans les expositions universelles et les jeux Olympiques. L'article retrace les débuts de l'histoire du Tekniska Museet et insiste sur le rôle de son premier directeur, Torsten Althin (1897-1982), et sur le besoin qu'éprouvait la Société des ingénieurs suédois de trouver un symbole à l'appui de leur reconnaissance sociale. Se basant sur les écrits du géographe suédois Torsten Hägerstrand (né en 1916), l'article introduit trois dichotomies: international/ national, contextuel / séquentiel, archéocentrique / contempocentrique. Il défend l'idée que tout musée de la technique peut être décrit en fonction de ces choix conceptuels.

Corporate Advertising, Public Relations and Popular Exhibits: The Case of Du Pont

David Rhees

This paper provides a case study of the public relations and advertising problems which prompted the Du Pont Company to sponsor popular exhibits in the late 1930s in the United States: convincing the public of the superiority of synthetic materials; shedding the company's image as a «Merchant of Death»; and combating anti-big bussiness sentiment. The paper demonstrates how these three concerns shaped a Du Pont Exhibit displayed at the New York Museum of Science and Industry and Philadelphia's Franklin Institute Science Museum in 1937-1938. Although Du Pont shifted its efforts to other kinds of advertising media after World War II, the negative publicity regarding chemicals during the 1980s has prompted renewed corporate interest in museums.

Cet article présente une étude des problèmes de relations publiques et de publicité qui ont amené la société Du Pont à sponsoriser des expositions dans les années 1930 aux Etats-Unis. Il fallait convaincre le public de la supériorité des matériaux synthétiques; effacer l'image de «marchand de mort» de la compagnie; et combattre le courant d'opinion qui s'opposait aux grands trusts. L'article montre comment ces trois préoccupations ont donné forme à une exposition de Du Pont au New York Museum of Science and Industry et au Philadelphia Franklin Institute en 1937-1938. Et bien que Du Pont ait concentré ses efforts sur d'autres sortes de supports publicitaires après la Seconde-Guerre mondiale, l'image négative des produits chimiques pendant les années 1980 a provoqué un regain de l'intérêt industriel pour les musées.

Celebration or Education? The Goals of the U.S. National Air and Space Museum

Alex Roland

The National Air and Space Museum (N.A.S.M.) of the United States is restoring for exhibition the *Enola Gay*, the aircraft that dropped the atomic bomb on Hiroshima at the end of World War Two. The project has stirred great controversy. Some argue that N.A.S.M. is a showcase of American achievement; to display the *Enola Gay* there is to appear to boast about an event that was solemn at best, shameful at worst. Others argue that the purpose of N.A.S.M. is to educate the public about historically significant events in American aviation and space history; however unpleasant its business may have been, this aircraft qualifies. This article examines the origins of N.A.S.M. in an attempt to determine what purpose its founders had in mind. The research finds evidence in support of both interpretations. By and large the staff at the Smithsonian came to favour education as the main goal, but Congress voted for celebration.

Le Musée national de l'air et de l'espace restaure aux fins d'exposition l'*Enola Gay*, l'avion qui à lancé la bombe atomique sur Hiroshima à la fin de la Seconde-Guerre mondiale. Le projet a suscité une grande controverse. D'aucuns voient dans le N.A.S.M. une vitrine de l'exploit américain; exposer l'*Enola Gay* à cet endroit reviendrait à se vanter d'un événement qui fut au mieux grave, au pire honteux. D'autres avancent que le rôle du N.A.S.M. est d'instruire le public au sujet des événements historiquement importants dans l'épopée de l'aviation américaine et de la conquête de l'espace; quelque déplaisant qu'ait été le travail, cet avion en fait partie. L'article examine les origines du N.A.S.M. dans le but de determiner quel objectifs ses fondateurs avaient en tête. Cette recherche donne raison aux deux interprètations: dans son ensemble, l'équipe du Smithsonian avait tendance à faire de l'éducation sa fonction première, mais le Congrès votait pour la célébration.

The New Generation of Museums: Technical, Industrial and "Ecomuseums"

Louis Bergeron

The history of the Museum located in Paris at the Conservatoire des Arts et Métiers (born 1794) shows that as soon as the middle of the XIXth century the idea of a Museum working as a «legal deposit» of all kind of machinery, growing indefinitely on the same premises, was an idea with no future. While its collections remain unvaluable and will enjoy a new presentation in the coming years, the very concept of technical and industrial museums has undergone deep changes over the past two decades in France. Their aims are getting more and more diversified and complexe : more specialized, devoted to particular industrial sectors or techniques, or connected with small geographical areas, these new museums are more interested in human know how and organization of the work than in industrial artefacts viewed exclusively as such. They should, too, add to conservation tasks an effort to radically improve the communication and enhance the presentation of collections by developing documentation and research about them.

L'histoire du musée logé au Conservatoire National des Arts et Métiers, fondé à Paris en 1794, montre que, dès le milieu du XIXe siècle, l'idée d'une musée fonctionnant comme «dépôt légal» de tous les types de machines, qui croîtrait indéfiniment dans les mêmes locaux, était sans avenir. Tandis que ses collections restent inestimables et s'apprêtent à connaitre une nouvelle présentation dans les prochaines années, la notion même de musée technique et industriel a subi de profonds changements au cours des deux dernières décennies. Les objectifs en deviennent de plus en plus diversifiés et complexes: plus spécialisés, consacrés à des secteurs industriels ou techniques spécifiques, ou créés en liaison avec de petites aires géographiques, ces nouveaux musées sont plus intéressés par le savoir-faire humain ou l'organisation du travail que par les artefacts industriels en tant que tels. Ils devraient aussi, outre leur devoir de conservation, s'efforcer d'améliorer radicalement leur communication et de mettre en valeur la présentation de leurs collections en développant documentation et recherche qui s'y rapportent.

History and Technology, 1993, Vol. 10, pp. 103-104
Reprint available directly from the publisher
Photocopying available by licence only

Index